IDEAL HOME

ENTERTAINING

ACKNOWLEDGEMENTS

*I would like to thank Caroline Waldegrave, Annie Harris and Emma Mann
without whom this book would not have happened. I would also like to thank Philippa Carr, MW, for
the wine recommendations throughout the book, and Judy Crawford and Sara Colquhoun for inspiration.
Thank you too to Madeline Weston, Emma Marsden and Tessa Clark for proof-reading,
Jane Coney for design, and to the students and teachers at Leith's School of Food and Wine for
testing recipes and helping with the food styling.
Last but not least I would like to thank my family for their continuing
enthusiasm for my experiments.*

FIRST PUBLISHED IN 1999 BY BOXTREE, AN IMPRINT OF MACMILLAN PUBLISHERS LTD,
25 ECCLESTON PLACE, LONDON, SW1W 9NF AND BASINGSTOKE
ASSOCIATED COMPANIES THROUGHOUT THE WORLD

ISBN 0 7522 2395 X

TEXT COPYRIGHT © 1999 SUSAN SPAULL

ALL PHOTOGRAPHY © MARTIN BRIGDALE,
EXCEPT: PAGES 56, 117, 133, 137, 177 LAURIE EVANS;
PAGES 109, 140, 184 © GRAHAM KIRK;
PAGE 172 © GUS FILGATE.
ALL FOOD STYLING BY HELEN TRENT,
EXCEPT PAGES 56, 109, 117, 133, 137, 140, 177 BY ANNIE HARRIS;
PAGE 172 BY DAVID JENKINS;
PAGE 184 BY GILLIAN MACLAURIN.
HOME ECONOMIST SUSAN SPAULL.

1 3 5 7 9 8 6 4 2

A CIP CATALOGUE RECORD FOR THIS BOOK IS AVAILABLE FROM THE BRITISH LIBRARY

COLOUR REPRODUCTION BY AYLESBURY STUDIOS LTD, BROMLEY, KENT
PRINTED BY BUTLER & TANNER, FROME, SOMERSET

IDEAL HOME IS PUBLISHED BY IPC MAGAZINES LTD, KING'S REACH TOWER, STAMFORD STREET, LONDON SE1 9LS.
FOR SUBSCRIPTION ENQUIRIES AND OVERSEAS ORDERS CALL 01444 445555 (FAX 01444 445599). PLEASE SEND ALL CORRESPONDENCE TO:
IPC MAGAZINES LTD, OAKFIELD HOUSE, 35 PERRYMOUNT ROAD, HAYWARDS HEATH, WEST SUSSEX RH16 3DH.
ALTERNATIVELY YOU CAN CALL THE SUBSCRIPTION CREDIT CARD HOTLINE (UK ORDERS ONLY) ON: 01622 778778.

IDEAL HOME
ENTERTAINING

SUSAN SPAULL

B☙XTREE

CONTENTS

INTRODUCTION

As a working mother with young children, my life is incredibly busy. I teach cookery at Leith's School of Food and Wine in London, in addition to testing and writing recipes for Ideal Home magazine, and as a result, I often find I have little time or energy to cook for my family and friends. The recipes in Ideal Home Entertaining are the recipes I rely upon when cooking at home. They can be prepared in advance, when I have time, then stored safely in the refrigerator or freezer until needed. Each recipe provides guidance on storing, presentation and serving, and a suggestion for the most appropriate wine.

Fortunately for busy people, entertaining in the 1990s has evolved from a formal affair requiring weeks of planning and days of hard work in the kitchen into a more spontaneous, relaxed occasion. Today we are comfortable serving a simpler style of food when entertaining. Formality is reserved for very special occasions.

Ideal Home Entertaining provides the recipes needed for today's entertaining with ideas for both informal and more formal occasions – and the flexibility of preparing the food when time is available. Cooks no longer want to spend days shopping and cooking only to find that they are too exhausted to enjoy entertaining. The availability of excellent prepared food means there is certainly no need to feel guilty about supplementing the menu with something delicious bought from a shop or a product that will save cooking time.

That said, I do love to cook. From the time I started testing mud pie recipes in my secret kitchen under the big fir tree in my garden, I realised I was happiest when I was measuring, mixing and experimenting with a new recipe. Cooking for me is relaxing and all engrossing. However, I do realise that many people find it very stressful, a chore rather than a pleasure. The recipes in this book have been tested many times, in home kitchens, to ensure the results are achievable and delicious. And as choosing what to cook can often take as long as the preparation, the section on Menu Planning provides an organised approach to planning a meal.

In food terms, I can think of nowhere else in the world more exciting than London. The variety of food and cultural influences that is part of our lives is tremendous. The 1990s have heralded an explosion of interest in good food. Cookery programmes on television have introduced new produce and foreign cuisine to all of us. These ingredients are now available across the country, either from local shops or specialist mail-order suppliers. Even ready-meals have done their part in educating us about different tastes, and the increasing popularity of organic produce and food from specialist suppliers reflects the fact that good ingredients are vital to producing delicious food. This growing interest in food and cookery is evident in the large range to be found in every supermarket.

In *Ideal Home Entertaining*, fresh seasonal ingredients and classic cookery techniques from around the world are combined to produce enticing, flavourful dishes which can be produced with confidence by anyone, from the novice cook to the experienced chef. In addition to providing an innovative twist to many of our British and French classics, these recipes reflect the influences of the Mediterranean, Asia and the Middle East. Most of the ingredients required can be found in any major supermarket, however a list of specialist suppliers for some unusual ingredients can be found at the end of the book.

I hope that you will enjoy cooking the recipes in this book as much as I do – and that you might even find cooking to be relaxing and enjoyable and as much fun as having your friends round for a meal.

HOW TO USE THE RECIPES

1 • Follow one set of measurements. Do not mix metric and imperial.

2 • Eggs are medium size, approximately 60–65 g (2½ oz) in weight.

3 • All spoon measures are level. 1 tbsp = 1 tablespoon. 1tsp = 1 teaspoon.

4 • All herbs are fresh unless specified otherwise. Use half the quantity of dried herbs if necessary.

5 • 1 pint = 20 fl oz.

6 • Ovens vary in the distribution of heat and time taken to complete cooking, so temperatures given are for guidance only. Recipes that suggest placing the food in the top third of the oven, as with pastries and breads for example, assume that the top is the hottest part. In America, the bottom of the oven is usually the hottest. It is best to check the manufacturer's directions if you are unsure.

PREPARING AHEAD

Cooking good food for family and friends undoubtly requires time and commitment, but it can be achieved by even the busiest person through careful planning and choice of recipe. To help with planning, preparation and cooking times are given with every recipe, as well as the length of time each recipe can be made in advance.

Remember to combine tasks where possible. For example, while the main course is in the oven prepare the first course or dessert. The dining table can often be laid several days in advance. Flowers are usually best arranged a few days ahead so that the blooms are at their peak. Delegate tasks whenever possible in order to avoid the stress of last-minute preparations.

MENU PLANNING

Planning a menu that is exciting and delicious but won't take an army of cooks to execute can be as difficult as the preparation. My mind often goes blank when confronted with planning a menu and I quietly start to panic.

To get over this initial hurdle I have designed a formula for menu planning. Starting with the main course ask youself these questions:

1 • WHAT IS THE SEASON?
Seasonal produce will always taste better and be less expensive than food that is out of season.

2 • WHAT IS THE OCCASION?
The style of the dish should complement the style of the occasion.

3 • HOW MANY PEOPLE AM I COOKING FOR?
Is it possible to make this dish for this number of people? Keep in mind the size of your kitchen and your own capabilities when it comes to cooking and serving.

4 • WHO AM I COOKING FOR?
What type of food do they like and how hungry are they likely to be? Are there any special diets to be catered for?

When you have decided on a main course dish, consider what dish you would like to have for a first course. This should complement the main course without duplicating flavours, ingredients, colour or texture. It should not have stronger flavours than the main course or be from a greatly different ethnic cusine. The first course should also satisfy the points above.

Now that you have planned the first and main course, try to imagine what you would like to have for dessert. Your choice should take all these points into consideration.

CHAPTER ONE

SOUPS

RED PEPPER AND PARSNIP SOUP

SERVES 6

40 g (1½ oz) butter

175 g (6 oz) onion, chopped

3 tbsp brandy

3 red peppers, de-seeded and chopped

675 g (1½ lb) parsnips, grated

2 ltr (3½ pt) chicken or vegetable stock

Salt and ground black pepper

PISTOU

55 g (2 oz) freshly grated Parmesan cheese

55 g (2 oz) fresh basil

1 clove garlic, crushed

150 ml (¼ pt) olive oil

Salt and ground black pepper

Spicy red peppers and sweet parsnips marry well to make a creamy soup.

Melt the butter in a heavy saucepan, stir in the onion and brandy, place a piece of damp greaseproof paper on the onion and cover with a lid. Cook over a low heat for 15 minutes or until the onion is softened but not browned. Remove the lid and paper.

Add the peppers, stir and cook for a further 5 minutes, then add the parsnips. Stir and cook for a further 5 minutes before adding the stock. Bring to the boil, cover and simmer for 20 minutes or until the vegetables are tender.

Let the soup cool a little, then purée until smooth, and season with salt and pepper.

For the pistou, put the Parmesan, basil and garlic into a food processor and, on a slow setting, add the oil while processing to a thick paste. Add 2 tbsp of hot soup and season.

Serve the soup either hot or chilled with 1 tsp of the pistou swirled into each serving.

380 CALS PER PORTION • 29 G FAT PER PORTION •PREPARATION TIME: 20 MIN • COOKING TIME: 45 MIN • CAN BE MADE 2 DAYS AHEAD • FREEZE-ABILITY: 2 MONTHS.

BUTTERNUT SQUASH AND LEEK SOUP

SERVES 6

675 g (1½ lb) leeks

450 g (1 lb) butternut squash

2 tbsp olive oil

5 tbsp dry Madeira or sherry

1.5 ltr (2½ pt) chicken or vegetable stock

Salt and ground black pepper

Lemon juice

100 g (3½ oz) crème fraîche

Grated nutmeg, to garnish

This hearty soup makes a quick lunch with crusty herb bread. Fresh pumpkin can be substituted for the squash.

Trim the roots and tough green tops from the leeks, slice finely, wash thoroughly and drain. Peel and de-seed the squash and cut into 2.5 cm (1 in) chunks.

Heat the oil in a large, heavy-based saucepan and stir in the leeks. Place a piece of damp greaseproof paper on the surface of the leeks, cover with a lid and cook over medium-low heat for 7 to 8 minutes until softened, then remove the paper and lid and pour in the wine. Let it boil for 2 minutes then add the squash and stock. Cover with a lid and simmer for about 15 minutes or until the squash is soft.

Let the soup cool a little, then purée until smooth. Season with salt, pepper and a squeeze of lemon juice.

To serve, reheat the soup and top each serving with a spoonful of crème fraîche and a little grated nutmeg.

140 CALS PER PORTION • 10 G FAT PER PORTION • PREPARATION TIME: 10 MIN • COOKING TIME: 30 MIN • CAN BE MADE 2 DAYS AHEAD • FREEZE-ABILITY: 2 MONTHS.

TIGER PRAWN, CELERIAC

AND APPLE SOUP

Peel and de-vein the prawns and store in the fridge until you need them. Put the prawn shells in a saucepan with the wine, leek, bay leaf, peppercorns and 1.2 ltr (2 pt) water. Simmer for 30 minutes to make a light stock.

Melt the butter in a large saucepan, stir in the onion, cover with a piece of damp greaseproof paper and a lid, and cook for 5 minutes or until soft. Remove the paper and lid, stir in the garlic, celeriac, apple and potato and strain the prawn-shell stock over the vegetables. Bring to simmering point, cover and cook for 25 minutes or until the vegetables are very soft.

Cool the soup, then purée with the crème fraîche until smooth. Return to the rinsed-out pan and adjust the seasoning. While the soup is gently reheating, heat the oil in a small pan over a medium-high heat and sauté the prawns, stirring, until they are bright pink and have curled. Ladle the soup into warmed serving bowls and top with the prawns and a sprinkling of dill.

234 CALS PER PORTION • 15 G FAT PER PORTION • PREPARATION TIME: 10 MIN •
COOKING TIME: 35 MIN • CAN BE MADE A DAY AHEAD • FREEZE-ABILITY: 2 MONTHS.

SERVES 6

225 g (8 oz) raw tiger prawns

150 ml ($\frac{1}{4}$ pt) dry white wine

1 leek, washed and thinly sliced

1 bay leaf

6 peppercorns

55 g (2 oz) butter

225 g (8 oz) onion, chopped

1 clove garlic, crushed

560 g (1$\frac{1}{4}$ lb) bulb of celeriac, peeled and grated

1 red dessert apple, cored and grated

110 g (4 oz) floury potato, peeled and grated

100 g (3$\frac{1}{2}$ oz) crème fraîche

Salt and ground black pepper

2 tsp oil

2 tbsp chopped fresh dill, to garnish

This sophisticated soup is easy to make the day it's to be served. It can be reheated and garnished at the last minute with the prawns which flavour the soup stock.

WINE TIP

Australian Semillon Chardonnay

ICED PEA AND MINT SOUP

WITH HOT CHILLI PRAWNS

Place the oil in a saucepan over a low heat. Stir in the onion, cover with a piece of damp greaseproof paper and a lid, and cook gently over a low heat for about 15 minutes, stirring occasionally until the onion has softened. Remove the lid and paper.

Add the potato, stock and seasoning and bring to the boil. Stir in the peas and simmer for about 20 minutes until tender.

To make the chilli prawns, de-seed and finely chop the chilli and stir into the prawns with the oil. Chill until required.

Allow the soup mixture to cool, then add half the cream. Purée, then push through a sieve. Finely chop the mint and add to the soup. Chill until required.

To serve, pre-heat the grill or barbecue. Thread the prawns on to skewers, then cook for 1 to 2 minutes on each side. They will turn bright pink and start to curl when ready.

Divide the soup between the bowls, drizzle a little of the remaining cream on top and divide the prawns equally. Garnish with the reserved sprigs of mint and serve.

217 CALS PER PORTION • 14 G FAT PER PORTION • PREPARATION TIME: 10 MIN •
COOKING TIME: 45 MIN • CAN BE MADE A DAY AHEAD • FREEZE-ABILITY: 1 MONTH.

SERVES 8

2 tbsp olive oil

1 medium onion, finely chopped

255 g (9 oz) floury potato, peeled
    and grated

1 ltr (1³/₄ pt) chicken or vegetable stock

Salt and ground black pepper

500 g (1 lb 2 oz) small green peas

150 ml (¹/₄ pt) double cream

15 g (¹/₂ oz) fresh mint (reserve 8 sprigs
    to garnish)

HOT CHILLI PRAWNS

1 small red chilli

285 g (10 oz) raw tiger prawns,
    peeled and de-veined

1 tbsp olive oil

Full of garden-fresh flavours, this soup can be served either warm or refreshingly cold.

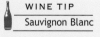
WINE TIP
Sauvignon Blanc

SPINACH AND LENTIL SOUP

WITH SAFFRON CREAM

SERVES 6

110 g (4 oz) green lentils

2 tbsp olive oil

225 g (8 oz) onion, chopped

Pinch of saffron strands

1 tsp ground coriander

$\frac{1}{2}$ tsp ground cumin

340 g (12 oz) fresh spinach, or 170 g
(6 oz) frozen spinach

500 ml (18 fl oz) chicken or
vegetable stock

Salt and ground black pepper

100 ml (3$\frac{1}{2}$ fl oz) Greek yoghurt

Healthy ingredients
combine to make this
beautifully green soup.

WINE TIP

Australian
Chardonnay

Put the lentils in a saucepan and cover with 500 ml (18 fl oz) water. Boil rapidly with the lid off for 10 minutes, then reduce the heat, cover and simmer for 15 minutes.

Place the olive oil in another saucepan and stir in the chopped onion. Cover with a piece of damp greaseproof paper on the onions and cover with a lid. Cook over a low heat for about 15 minutes, until the onion is soft.

Meanwhile, place the saffron in a small bowl and pour over 2 tbsp of boiling water. Set aside.

When the onion is soft, remove the lid and greaseproof paper and add the coriander and cumin. Stir over a medium heat for 1 minute.

Add the spinach and cook until wilted. Add the mixture to the lentils with the stock. Simmer for 5 minutes. Cool, then liquidise until smooth.

To serve, reheat the soup until steaming hot, but not boiling, and season to taste. Stir the saffron into the Greek yoghurt and drizzle over each bowl of soup.

140 CALS PER PORTION • 6 G FAT PER PORTION • PREPARATION TIME: 10 MIN • COOKING TIME: 30 MIN • CAN BE MADE 2 DAYS AHEAD • FREEZE-ABILITY: 2 MONTHS.

WATERCRESS AND SPINACH SOUP

Melt the butter in a saucepan and stir in the onion. Place a piece of damp grease-proof paper on the surface of the onion, cover with a lid and cook over a low heat for 15 minutes until softened. Remove the lid and paper.

Stir in the potatoes and vegetable stock and simmer for 10 minutes until the potato is soft. Meanwhile, wash the watercress and spinach, then discard any thick stems, and roughly chop.

Add the watercress and spinach to the pan, then stir and simmer for 3 minutes until the leaves are wilted. Leave to cool.

Purée the soup in a liquidiser until smooth and gently reheat. Add the nutmeg and seasoning. Transfer to serving bowls, swirl in the cream and serve with Cheddar Muffins (see recipe on page 181).

162 CALS PER PORTION • 13 G FAT PER PORTION • PREPARATION TIME: 5 MIN • COOKING TIME: 30 MIN • CAN BE MADE 2 DAYS AHEAD • FREEZE-ABILITY: 2 MONTHS.

SERVES 8

30 g (1 oz) butter

225 g (8 oz) onion, chopped

285 g (10 oz) floury potatoes, peeled and grated

1 ltr (1¾ pt) vegetable stock

140 g (5 oz) watercress

200 g (7 oz) fresh spinach

Freshly grated nutmeg

Salt and ground black pepper

150 ml (¼ pt) double cream

The watercress makes this brilliant green soup enticingly peppery.

WINE TIP
New Zealand
Sauvignon Blanc

This intensely flavoured soup makes the most of ripe tomatoes.

ROASTED TOMATO SOUP

WITH BASIL CREAM

SERVES 6

1 kg (2¹/₄ lb) ripe, plum tomatoes
2 large red onions
3 rosemary sprigs
2 tbsp balsamic vinegar
1 tsp caster sugar
2 tbsp olive oil
1 ltr (1³/₄ pt) vegetable or chicken stock
2 tbsp Madeira
Basil sprigs, to garnish
BASIL CREAM
15 g (¹/₂ oz) fresh basil
100 ml (3¹/₂ fl oz) single cream

WINE TIP
Riesling

Pre-heat the oven to 200°C, 400°F, Gas 6. Cut the tomatoes in half and place cut-side up in an ovenproof dish.

Peel the red onions and cut into eighths. Place in a single layer in the ovenproof dish with the tomatoes. Tuck the rosemary sprigs under the vegetables, sprinkle over the balsamic vinegar, caster sugar and oil, then roast in the oven for 1 hour, or until the vegetables have softened and browned.

Transfer the vegetables to a large saucepan, cover with the stock and Madeira, and simmer over a medium heat for 30 minutes, or until the vegetables start to disintegrate.

To make the basil cream, plunge the fresh basil into boiling water for 10 seconds, then refresh under cold water. Pat the leaves dry and liquidise with the single cream.

Liquidise the soup, then pass through a sieve. Gently warm the soup and transfer to serving bowls. Drizzle the basil cream over the top, garnish with basil sprigs and serve immediately.

168 CALS PER PORTION • 12 G FAT PER PORTION • PREPARATION TIME: 15 MIN •
COOKING TIME: 1¹/₂ HR • CAN BE MADE 2 DAYS AHEAD • FREEZE-ABILITY: 2 MONTHS.

CHEAT'S WILD MUSHROOM RISOTTO

Pour 150 ml (¼ pt) boiling water over the dried mushrooms and leave to soak for 20 minutes.

Pre-heat the oven to 150°C, 300°F, Gas 2. Heat the butter and oil in a large saucepan and stir in the onion. Place a piece of damp greaseproof paper on the onion, then cover with a lid and cook over a low heat for 15 to 20 minutes until very soft.

Using a potato peeler, make 8 tbsp of Parmesan shavings, and finely grate the remaining cheese. Set both aside.

Remove the lid and paper from the onion, stir in the garlic and chestnut or button mushrooms and cook for 5 minutes.

Drain the porcini mushrooms, adding the liquid to the chicken stock, then slice and add to the pan with the Madeira.

Stir in the rice and salt, then add the stock and bring to a simmer. Transfer to a large ovenproof dish, cover with foil and cook in the oven for 30 minutes, stirring occasionally and adding more stock as necessary as the rice absorbs the liquid. If making ahead, stop cooking at this stage and cool completely before chilling.

To finish bake the risotto for a further 20 minutes, or 35 minutes if cooking from cold. About 5 minutes before serving, stir in the grated Parmesan and season with pepper. Garnish with the Parmesan shavings and chopped parsley.

284 CALS PER PORTION • 14 G FAT PER PORTION • PREPARATION TIME: 30 MIN •
COOKING TIME: 50 MIN • CAN BE MADE A DAY AHEAD • FREEZE-ABILITY: NOT ADVISABLE.

SERVES 8

30 g (1 oz) dried porcini mushrooms

55 g (2 oz) butter

2 tbsp olive oil

1 large onion, finely chopped

110 g (4 oz) piece of Parmesan cheese

1 clove garlic, crushed

255 g (9 oz) chestnut or
   button mushrooms, sliced

1.2 ltr (2 pt) hot chicken stock

2 tbsp dry Madeira

255 g (9 oz) risotto rice

1 tsp salt

Freshly ground black pepper

2 tbsp chopped fresh parsley, to garnish

This method takes the last-minute hassle out of making risotto.

WINE TIP
Chianti

This light first course is quick to make and deliciously simple.

GRILLED SCALLOPS WITH

CHILLI AND GARLIC

SERVES 8

30 g (1 oz) butter

340 g (12 oz) fresh baby spinach, washed

Salt and ground black pepper

500 g (1 lb 2 oz) fresh scallops

1 tbsp olive oil

Juice of ½ lemon

1 clove garlic, roasted (see Cook's Tip below) and crushed

1 red chilli, de-seeded and finely diced

2 tbsp fresh white breadcrumbs

1 tbsp melted butter

WINE TIP
Alsace Pinot Gris

Melt the butter in a large sauté pan over a medium-high heat. When the butter starts to brown, tip the wet spinach into the pan and sauté quickly, turning it with two wooden spoons. Remove the spinach from the pan as soon as it wilts and place in a sieve to drain and cool.

Place the spinach in a shallow ovenproof dish and season well.

Remove any membrane from the edges of the scallops. The roe can be cooked or removed as desired.

Toss the scallops with the oil, lemon juice, garlic and chilli (reserving some chilli to garnish), then place on top of the spinach.

Mix the breadcrumbs and melted butter and sprinkle over the scallops. Place under a hot grill for 5 to 10 minutes, until the scallops are opaque and firm to the touch and the breadcrumbs are golden brown. Sprinkle with the reserved chilli and serve.

COOK'S TIP • To roast garlic, place individual cloves in a ramekin in the oven at 180°C, 350°F, Gas 4 for 10 minutes, or until tender when pierced with a skewer.

133 CALS PER PORTION • 7 G FAT PER PORTION • PREPARATION TIME: 15 MIN •
COOKING TIME: 10 MIN • CAN BE ASSEMBLED A DAY AHEAD • FREEZE-ABILITY: CANNOT BE FROZEN.

OYSTERS ROCKEFELLER

Split the oysters using a shucker or small knife, leaving each one in its rounded half-shell with the juice.

Sprinkle a 1 cm (½ in) thick layer of coarse salt on to two baking sheets. Nestle the oysters in their half-shells on the salt and chill until required (no longer than 24 hours).

Pre-heat the oven to 230°C, 450°F, Gas 8. Remove the large stalks from the spinach and watercress, and wash well.

Melt 15 g (½ oz) of the butter in a pan over a high heat. Sauté the spinach and watercress for 2 minutes until the leaves wilt. Drain and cool.

Squeeze dry the spinach and watercress, then place in a food processor with the remaining ingredients, except the oysters. Blend until smooth.

Place 1 tsp of the spinach mixture on top of each oyster, then bake for 8 to 10 minutes until bubbling. Serve with crusty bread.

116 CALS PER PORTION • 7 G FAT PER PORTION • PREPARATION TIME: 20 MIN • COOKING TIME: 10 MIN • CAN BE MADE A DAY AHEAD • FREEZE-ABILITY: 1 WEEK FOR THE SPINACH MIXTURE.

SERVES 8

40 medium oysters
Coarse salt
255 g (9 oz) fresh spinach
1 bunch of fresh watercress
55 g (2 oz) butter, softened
30 g (1 oz) fresh breadcrumbs
1 celery stick, chopped
2 tbsp chopped fresh parsley
½ bunch of spring onions
2 tbsp Pernod
Tabasco sauce to taste
Salt and ground black pepper

This popular cooked oyster dish originated in New Orleans.

WINE TIP
Champagne

SALSA GRATINEED MUSSELS

SERVES 6

48 mussels or 30
green-lipped mussels

SALSA

1 tbsp olive oil

85 g (3 oz) onion, finely chopped

¹/₂ green pepper, finely chopped

1 clove garlic, crushed

2 green chillies, de-seeded and
finely diced

400 g (14 oz) can of chopped tomatoes
in tomato juice

2 tsp red wine vinegar

¹/₂ tsp caster sugar

2 tbsp chopped fresh coriander

Jalapeño sauce to taste

Salt and ground black pepper

GRATIN

55 g (2 oz) fresh brown breadcrumbs

30 g (1 oz) butter, melted

30 g (1 oz) Parmesan cheese,
freshly grated

3 limes, cut into quarters, to serve

To make the salsa, heat the oil in a small sauté pan. Add the onion and green pepper and cook until softened.

Stir in the garlic and chillies and cook for 1 minute, then stir in the remaining ingredients and heat gently for 2 minutes, crushing the tomatoes slightly with a wooden spoon. Season to taste, then leave to cool completely.

Wash the mussels, pulling off any beards and scraping barnacles off with a knife. Discard any open mussels which do not close when tapped, or any with broken shells.

To steam the mussels, fill a large sauté pan or saucepan with 2.5 cm (1 in) water. Boil the water and place the mussels in the pan. Cover, then steam for 2 to 3 minutes or until the shells are wide open. Discard any that haven't opened after steaming. Drain the mussels in a colander and cool completely.

Combine the ingredients for the gratin in a bowl. Remove the top shells from the cooled mussels, then coat each mussel with a layer of salsa and sprinkle over the gratin mixture. The mussels can be frozen or stored in the fridge for 24 hours.

To serve, grill the mussels for 5 minutes until brown. If cooking from frozen, pre-heat the oven to 220°C, 425°F, Gas 7, and bake the mussels for 10 minutes, or until they are piping hot and golden brown. Place 2 lime quarters on each serving plate and surround with the mussels.

165 CALS PER PORTION • 9 G FAT PER PORTION • PREPARATION TIME: 30 MIN •
COOKING TIME: 10 MIN • SALSA CAN BE MADE 1 WEEK AHEAD; MUSSELS CAN BE MADE A DAY AHEAD
• FREEZE-ABILITY: SALSA. 1 MONTH; MUSSELS. 1 MONTH.

These spicy mussels
are an ideal first course
before a spicy meal.
The salsa makes a great dip
for tortilla chips, too.

WINE TIP
Australian
Chardonnay

DOUBLE-BAKED SPINACH

AND SAGE SOUFFLES

Generously butter eight 150 ml (¼ pt) timbale moulds or ramekins.

Pre-heat the oven to 200°C, 400°F, Gas 6. Place a roasting tin half-filled with water (a bain-marie) in the oven. It should be large enough to hold all the moulds.

Heat the milk with the slice of onion until it steams. Turn off the heat. Leave to stand for about 10 minutes, then discard the onion.

Trim the stems from the spinach and discard. Blanch the leaves in a little boiling salted water until wilted, then drain. When cool, squeeze dry and finely chop.

Melt the butter in a clean saucepan and stir in the flour. Cook over a medium heat, stirring, for 1 minute. Remove the pan from heat and gradually add the milk, stirring until smooth.

Return the sauce to the heat and cook over a medium temperature, stirring until it thickens. Boil for 30 seconds, then leave to cool for 5 minutes.

Stir the sauce into the egg yolks, a little at a time. Stir in the spinach, Gruyère and chopped sage. Season well with nutmeg, salt and pepper.

Whisk the egg whites until just stiff, gently fold into the spinach mixture and spoon into the moulds. Place the moulds in the bain-marie and cook for 12 to 15 minutes, or until well risen and lightly browned on top.

Remove the soufflés from the oven and allow to stand and sink. Turn out into an ovenproof dish.

Pre-heat the oven to 220°C, 425°F, Gas 7. About 10 minutes before serving, pour the cream over the soufflés and sprinkle with the Parmesan cheese. Place the dish in the oven for 10 minutes or until the tops are lightly browned. Garnish with sage leaves and serve immediately.

240 CALS PER PORTION • 19 G FAT PER PORTION • PREPARATION TIME: 30 MIN •
COOKING TIME: 25 MIN • CAN BE MADE A DAY AHEAD • FREEZE-ABILITY: CANNOT BE FROZEN.

SERVES 8

Melted butter for greasing moulds
290 ml (½ pt) milk
1 slice of onion
200g (7 oz) fresh spinach
40 g (1½ oz) butter
40 g (1½ oz) plain flour
2 egg yolks, beaten
55 g (2 oz) Gruyère cheese, grated
½ tsp finely chopped fresh sage
Pinch of freshly grated nutmeg
Salt and ground black pepper
4 egg whites
150 ml (¼ pt) single cream
6 tbsp grated Parmesan cheese
Sage leaves, to garnish

The spinach makes these soufflés extra-light. The beauty of these soufflés is that they can be prepared and baked in advance then finished off when your guests arrive.

WINE TIP
Chilean
Sauvignon Blanc

GRILLED GOAT'S CHEESE

WITH PINK GOOSEBERRY CHUTNEY

To make the walnut bread croutes, pre-heat the grill and cut six 1 cm (½ in) thick slices from the loaf, removing the crusts. Cut the slices into rounds, each the same diameter as the goat's cheese. Brush the bread rounds with olive oil, then toast under the grill until lightly browned. If making ahead, cool, then store in an airtight container.

To make the dressing, place the vinegar in a small bowl and whisk in the mustard, then the oils. Season and store in the fridge if making ahead.

Pre-heat the grill. Cut the goat's cheese log into six rounds and place on the walnut bread croutes. Transfer to a baking sheet and place under the grill, as close as possible to the heat source, for about 2 minutes, or until the cheese starts to melt and browns slightly.

Toss the salad leaves with the dressing and divide between serving plates. Place a goat's cheese croute on each plate and serve with Pink Gooseberry Chutney (see recipe below).

372 CALS PER PORTION • 24 G FAT PER PORTION • PREPARATION TIME: 15 MIN •
COOKING TIME: 5 MIN • CAN BE MADE A DAY AHEAD • FREEZE-ABILITY: NOT ADVISABLE.

SERVES 6

1 loaf of walnut bread

1 tbsp olive oil

200 g (7 oz) goat's cheese log

200 g (7 oz) mixed salad leaves

DRESSING

1 tbsp raspberry vinegar

¼ tsp Dijon mustard

2 tbsp olive oil

1 tbsp sunflower oil

Salt and ground black pepper

Warm, melting goat's cheese with a fruity chutney is a popular first course at any time of year.

WINE TIP
Sancerre

PINK GOOSEBERRY CHUTNEY

Pre-heat the oven to 150°C, 300°F, Gas 2. Wash two jam jars and place them upside down on a rack in the oven until dry and very hot. Remove the jars from the oven using oven gloves.

Prepare the fruit by washing and removing any stones. Cut the gooseberries in half and the other fruit into similar-sized pieces.

Dissolve the sugar in the vinegar, then add the ginger, mustard seeds, cloves and cinnamon stick. Add the fruit and bring to the boil. Simmer gently for 15 minutes.

Strain the fruit, then reduce the liquid by boiling until syrupy. Stir the syrup into the fruit, pour into the clean jars and cover with jam seals.

139 CALS PER PORTION • 0.5 G FAT PER PORTION • PREPARATION TIME: 5 MIN •
COOKING TIME: 25 MIN • CAN BE MADE 2 MONTHS AHEAD • FREEZE-ABILITY: 6 MONTHS.

MAKES ABOUT 675 G (1½ LB)

255 g (9 oz) pink gooseberries

255 g (9 oz) other red fruit, such as
  plums, rhubarb, etc.

255 g (9 oz) granulated sugar

200 ml (7 fl oz) cider vinegar

½ tsp ground ginger

2 tsp mustard seeds

2 cloves

2.5 cm (1 in) cinnamon stick

This fruity chutney offsets the richness of the goat's cheese.

ASPARAGUS PARCELS

WITH LEMON HOLLANDAISE SAUCE

SERVES 8

1 kg (2¼ lb) fresh asparagus

2 tbsp olive oil

2 shallots, peeled and finely chopped

Juice of 1 lemon

HOLLANDAISE SAUCE

110 g (4 oz) unsalted butter

2 egg yolks

1 tbsp lemon juice

Salt and freshly ground white pepper

Roasting the asparagus in paper parcels captures the flavours. When the parcels are opened the wonderful aromas are released with the steam.

WINE TIP

Alsace Pinot Gris

Pre-heat the oven to 200°C, 400°F, Gas 6. Trim the woody stems from the asparagus and discard.

Fold eight 40 cm (16 in) squares of greaseproof paper in half, cut each into a half-heart shape, then open out and brush each paper heart with olive oil.

Place equal amounts of asparagus on one half of each paper heart. Sprinkle over the chopped shallots and lemon juice, then fold over the other side of the paper and roll the edges together, starting from the top, to seal. Place on a baking sheet and cook for 10 minutes or until the asparagus is tender when pierced with a knife.

To make the hollandaise sauce, heat the butter in a pan until just melted and warm.

Place the egg yolks and lemon juice in a liquidiser and whiz for 30 seconds. With the liquidiser running, add the warm butter in a thin stream. Season with salt and pepper, and more lemon juice, if liked.

Place the asparagus parcels on serving plates, unwrap and pour over the hollandaise sauce. Serve immediately.

167 CALS PER PORTION • 16 G FAT PER PORTION • PREPARATION TIME: 15 MIN •
COOKING TIME: 10 MIN • CAN BE MADE 2 HOURS AHEAD • FREEZE-ABILITY: CANNOT BE FROZEN.

CARROT AND CARDAMOM SOUFFLES

Pre-heat the oven to 200°C, 400°F, Gas 6, with a roasting tin half-filled with water (a bain marie) on the middle shelf.

Place the carrots in a saucepan with enough water to cover. Add 2 of the cardamom pods and the salt and caster sugar. Cover and cook for 10 minutes, until tender. Drain and cool. Discard the cardamon pods.

Place the milk, onion, ginger and remaining cardamom pods in a small saucepan. Heat until the milk steams, then leave to infuse for 10 minutes. Strain through a sieve, reserving the milk.

Melt the butter in a saucepan and use a little to brush the insides of six 150 ml (¼ pt) dariole moulds.

Stir the flour into the remaining butter with the ground cardamom to make a smooth paste. Cook over a medium heat for 1 minute. Remove and slowly stir in the milk to make a smooth sauce. Return to the heat, bring to the boil and cook for 1 minute.

Remove the sauce from the heat and stir in the cheeses, then the egg yolks. Place in a food processor with the chilli sauce and carrots, and process until smooth. Season.

Whisk the egg whites until stiff, then fold into the carrot mixture. Gently pile the mixture into the moulds, place in the bain marie and bake for 12 to 14 minutes, until the soufflés are well risen and lightly browned.

Remove the soufflés from the bain marie and allow to sink and cool slightly for about 5 minutes. Turn out into an ovenproof dish.

To make the caramelised pecans, heat the caster sugar in a heavy-based saucepan over a low heat. When the sugar has turned a dark amber colour, remove from the heat and add the pecans. Use a fork to turn the pecans over to coat them with caramel. Place on an oiled tray to harden. Store in an airtight container until required.

To make the sauce, blanch the watercress in boiling water for 10 seconds then refresh under cold running water. Roughly chop the leaves and liquidise in a blender with the single cream. Add seasoning to taste.

To serve, pre-heat the oven to 225°C, 425°F, Gas 7. Reheat the soufflés for 10 minutes. Warm the sauce. Transfer the soufflés to plates and serve immediately with the sauce and pecans. Garnish with the watercress leaves.

SERVES 6

- 225 g (8 oz) carrots, peeled and thinly sliced
- 4 cardamom pods, lightly crushed
- Pinch of salt
- Pinch of caster sugar
- 200 ml (7 fl oz) milk
- Slice of onion
- 1 cm (¼ in) piece of fresh ginger, peeled and sliced
- 40 g (1½ oz) butter
- 30 g (1 oz) plain flour
- ¼ tsp ground cardamom
- 30 g (1 oz) Gruyère cheese, finely grated
- 15 g (½ oz) Parmesan cheese, finely grated
- 2 egg yolks
- 1 tsp chilli sauce
- Salt and ground black pepper
- 3 egg whites
- Watercress leaves, to garnish

CARAMELISED PECANS
- 55 g (2 oz) caster sugar
- 55 g (2 oz) whole pecans

WATERCRESS SAUCE
- 1 bunch of watercress
- 150 ml (¼ pt) single cream
- Salt and ground black pepper

These colourful soufflés are an impressive start to a meal.

WINE TIP
Soave

320 CALS PER PORTION • 23 G FAT PER PORTION • PREPARATION TIME: 25 MIN •
COOKING TIME: 25 MIN • CAN BE MADE A DAY AHEAD • FREEZE-ABILITY: NOT ADVISABLE.

HOT FIRST COURSES   27

THAI-STYLE CRAB CAKES

SERVES 8

450 g (1 lb) cooked white fish, such
as whiting or cod

110g (4 oz) cooked white and brown crabmeat

225 g (8 oz) mashed potatoes, unseasoned

1 egg, beaten

1 tsp grated fresh ginger

1 clove garlic, crushed

1 tsp powdered lemongrass

1 tbsp fish sauce

2 tbsp chopped fresh coriander

Juice of $\frac{1}{2}$ lime

$\frac{1}{2}$ tsp salt

Freshly ground black pepper

COATING

55 g (2 oz) seasoned flour

2 eggs, beaten

140 g (5 oz) fresh white breadcrumbs, sieved

Oil for frying

Salt for sprinkling

Mix together the crab cake ingredients and shape into 16 rounds, 1.5 cm ($\frac{5}{8}$ in) thick. If you want to serve them as nibbles, divide the mixture into 50 mini cakes. Chill.

Coat each fish cake in the flour, then in the beaten egg and breadcrumbs. Shallow-fry in oil for 2 to 3 minutes on each side until golden. Drain, then sprinkle with a little salt. Transfer to plates, garnish with coriander and serve warm with the Sweet Chilli Sauce (see recipe below).

SWEET CHILLI SAUCE

150 ml ($\frac{1}{4}$ pt) white wine vinegar

3 red chillies, de-seeded and chopped

2 cloves garlic, crushed

110 g (4 oz) caster sugar

$\frac{1}{2}$ tsp salt

1 tbsp fish sauce

Combine all the ingredients in a liquidiser, then place in a saucepan over a low heat until all the sugar has dissolved. Cool.

Serve as a dipping sauce for fish or chicken.

THAI-STYLE CRAB CAKES WITH SWEET CHILLI SAUCE • 326 CALS PER PORTION • 11 G FAT PER PORTION •
PREPARATION TIME: 30 MIN • COOKING TIME: 20 MIN • CAN BE MADE A DAY AHEAD •
FREEZE-ABILITY: 1 MONTH FOR THAI CRAB CAKES. NOT ADVISABLE FOR SAUCE.

BRULEED CRAB TARTLETS

SERVES 8

30 g (1 oz) butter

2 shallots, finely chopped

30g (1 oz) plain flour

Strip of lemon zest

290 ml (1/2 pt) milk

1 egg, seperated

1 tbsp snipped fresh chives

225 g (8 oz) cooked white crabmeat,
picked over and flaked

Salt and ground white pepper

Lemon juice to taste

55 g (2 oz) hollandaise sauce
(see recipe on page 26)

Salad leaves, to garnish

PASTRY

225 g (8 oz) plain flour

1/2 tsp of salt

30 g (1 oz) white vegetable fat

85 g (3 oz) firm butter

4 to 5 tbsp ice-cold water

Crab makes a luxurious tart
for a special occasion.
Other kinds of fish can be
substituted, if desired.

WINE TIP
Sauvignon Blanc

To make the pastry, sieve the flour and salt into a bowl. Cut in the fat using two knives, scissor fashion, then rub with your fingertips until the mixture resembles breadcrumbs. Using a table knife, stir in enough water to bring the dough together. Line eight 10 cm (4 in) tins with the pastry. Chill in the fridge until firm.

Pre-heat the oven to 200°C, 400°F, Gas 6. Line the tart cases with greasproof paper and enough baking beans to support the sides of the pastry and just cover the base. Place on a baking sheet and bake in the top third of the oven for 15 minutes then remove the beans and paper. Bake for a further 10 minutes or until the pastry is a light golden brown. Cool on a wire rack. Reduce the oven temperature to 160°C, 325°F, Gas 3.

Melt the butter in a small saucepan and cook the shallots until soft. Stir in the flour and cook for 1 minute. Add the lemon zest. Add the milk slowly then bring to the boil whilst stirring. Boil for 1 minute then cool for 5 minutes.

Remove the zest from the sauce and beat in the egg yolk. Stir in the chives and crabmeat and season with the salt, pepper and lemon juice. Whisk the egg white and fold into the mixture. Turn into the pastry cases. Bake for 15 minutes. The fillings should be slightly wobbly.

If you are preparing ahead the tarts can be stored in the fridge for up to 1 day. To reheat, place the tarts in a 200°C, 400°F, Gas 6 oven for 10 minutes, then grill.

Pre-heat the grill. Spoon a thin layer of the hollandaise sauce over the tarts. Place under the grill for about 1 minute until well browned. Garnish with salad leaves.

430 CALS PER PORTION • 25 G FAT PER PORTION • PREPARATION TIME: 30 MIN • COOKING TIME: 45 MIN • CAN BE MADE A DAY AHEAD • FREEZE-ABILITY: NOT ADVISABLE.

GRILLED VEGETABLE AND GOAT'S CHEESE STACKS WITH BASIL VINAIGRETTE

To make the vinaigrette, blend the vinegar, mustard and salt in a liquidiser. Slowly add the oil with the machine running.

Reserving some of the basil sprigs for garnish, add the remainder to the liquidiser, season with pepper and process until smooth. Chill until required.

Cut the aubergines into 5 mm (¼ in) thick slices. Sprinkle with a little salt, then press between two plates and leave for 30 minutes to allow the bitter juices to run out.

Remove and discard the cores and seeds from the peppers and cut into quarters. Cook under a hot grill until the skins are blackened, then place in a plastic bag until cool.

Cut the courgettes into 3 mm (⅛ in) slices. Brush with a little of the vinaigrette, then cook on a hot griddle for 1 minute each side. Set aside.

Dry the aubergines, then brush with a little vinaigrette. Cook on a hot griddle for 2 minutes on each side. Set aside.

Peel the skins from the peppers and discard. Cut into rounds using a scone-cutter or kitchen scissors.

Cut the tomatoes into 0.5 cm (¼ in) thick slices and layer with the other vegetables and goat's cheese into eight stacks. Chill until required.

Pre-heat the oven to 200°C, 400°F, Gas 6. Cook the vegetable stacks for 5 minutes until warmed through. Garnish with the reserved basil and serve with the remaining vinaigrette and Red Onion Focaccia (see recipe on page 182).

236 CALS PER PORTION • 21 G FAT PER PORTION • PREPARATION TIME: 1 HR • COOKING TIME: 5 MIN • CAN BE MADE A DAY AHEAD • FREEZE-ABILITY: CANNOT BE FROZEN.

SERVES 8

2 aubergines, each weighing 225 g (8 oz)
Salt
2 large red peppers
2 large yellow peppers
2 medium courgettes
2 large tomatoes
140 g (5 oz) soft goat's cheese
VINAIGRETTE
2 tbsp white wine vinegar
1 tsp Dijon mustard
½ tsp salt
150 ml (¼ pt) olive oil
8 basil sprigs
Freshly ground black pepper

Warming the vegetables before serving makes this first course suitable for any time of the year.

WINE TIP
Italian Dolcetto

OVERLEAF • GRILLED VEGETABLE AND GOAT'S CHEESE STACKS WITH BASIL VINAIGRETTE

CHAPTER THREE

COLD FIRST COURSES

HERB CHEESE AND CUCUMBER PATE

SERVES 6

1 tsp powdered gelatine

1 cucumber, peeled and de-seeded

1 tsp salt

1 tsp caster sugar

2 tbsp white wine vinegar

500 g (1 lb 2 oz) curd cheese

150 ml (¼ pt) Greek yoghurt

1 clove garlic, crushed

1 tbsp chopped fresh mint

5 spring onions, finely chopped

Freshly ground black pepper

Salad leaves, to serve

The flavours of this quick-to-make pâté are reminiscent of the Greek dip tzatziki. For vegetarians, substitute ½ tsp agar dissolved in 2 tbsp boiling water for the gelatine.

WINE TIP
Sauvignon Blanc

Lightly oil six 150 ml (¼ pt) ramekins and line with clingfilm. Place 2 tbsp cold water in a small saucepan and sprinkle the powdered gelatine over the top. Set aside.

Finely dice half the cucumber and cut the remainder into strips. Place the diced cucumber in a sieve over a bowl and sprinkle with half the salt, caster sugar and vinegar. Allow to stand.

Place the cucumber strips in a bowl and sprinkle with the remaining salt, sugar and vinegar. Chill until required.

Beat the curd cheese until smooth, then stir in the Greek yoghurt, garlic, mint and spring onions. Season to taste with pepper.

Melt the gelatine over a low heat, then stir into the cheese mixture. Drain the diced cucumber, pat dry with kitchen paper and stir into the cheese.

Turn the mixture into the prepared ramekins and cover with clingfilm. Chill for at least 4 hours or up to 2 days. Turn the pâté out of the ramekins on to plates, garnish with cucumber strips and serve with the salad leaves and wholemeal bread or rolls.

187 CALS PER PORTION • 12 G FAT PER PORTION • PREPARATION TIME: 20 MIN PLUS 4 HR CHILLING TIME • CAN BE MADE 2 DAYS AHEAD • FREEZE-ABILITY: CANNOT BE FROZEN.

ROASTED AUBERGINE AND AVOCADO

DIP WITH PITTA BREAD CRISPS

Pre-heat the oven to 200°C, 400°F, Gas 6. Rub the aubergine with oil and place in a roasting tin in the oven.

After 20 minutes, place the whole garlic cloves under the aubergine in the tin and continue to roast for 20 minutes. Remove from the oven and allow to cool.

Meanwhile, make the pitta bread crisps. Divide each pitta bread into two flat halves, brush with a little oil and sprinkle with the garlic salt. Cut each piece into 5 cm (2½ in) triangles.

Place the pitta bread on a baking sheet and cook in the oven for 5 minutes or until golden brown. Cool on a wire rack and store in an airtight container for up to 1 week.

Slit the cooled aubergine in half and scoop out the flesh, placing it in a large bowl or processor.

Peel the garlic cloves and add to the aubergine, along with the avocado flesh and lemon juice. Mash or pulse until just combined.

Stir in the crème fraîche and chopped parsley, then season and chill until required. Garnish with parsley sprigs and serve with the pitta bread crisps and salad leaves.

387 CALS PER PORTION • 20 G FAT PER PORTION • PREPARATION TIME: 10 MIN • COOKING TIME: 40 MIN •
CAN BE MADE A DAY AHEAD • FREEZE-ABILITY: CANNOT BE FROZEN.

SERVES 6

340 g (12 oz) aubergine
A little olive oil
2 cloves garlic, unpeeled
1 ripe avocado
2 tbsp lemon juice
110 g (4 oz) crème fraîche
1 tbsp chopped fresh parsley
Salt and ground black pepper
Flat-leaf parsley sprigs, to garnish
Salad leaves, to serve
PITTA BREAD CRISPS
6 pieces of pitta bread
Olive oil for brushing
Garlic salt

Fragrant with garlic and lemons, this easy-to-make dip is ideal for informal gatherings of friends.

WINE TIP
Chardonnay

QUICK SEAFOOD PATE

SERVES 6 8

110 g (4 oz) cooked medium prawns

200 g (7 oz) cooked crabmeat

200 g (7 oz) cooked, skinned and
boned salmon

110 g (4 oz) butter, melted and cooled

Grated zest and juice of 1 lemon

175 g (6 oz) fresh white breadcrumbs

290 ml (½ pt) single cream

1 tsp creamed horseradish

1 tbsp snipped fresh chives

Salt and ground black pepper

Dill sprigs and unshelled cooked prawns,
to garnish

Lemon wedges, to serve

Serve this pâté whole as
an addition to your buffet
table or cut into slices and
serve on individual plates. In
order to hold its shape, this
pâté must be frozen, then
defrosted before serving.

WINE TIP
German Riesling

Line a 20 x 10 cm (8 x 4 in) loaf tin with clingfilm. Arrange about 10 of the prawns along the base of the tin and chop the remainder.

Flake the crabmeat and salmon and mix in the chopped prawns and all the remaining ingredients except the garnish and lemon wedges. Season to taste, then spread the mixture in the loaf tin and press down firmly. Cover with clingfilm and foil and freeze for a minimum of 12 hours (or up to a month).

Defrost in the fridge overnight. Turn out of the tin and remove the lining film. Garnish with sprigs of dill and unshelled prawns. Serve with lemon wedges and brown bread and butter.

488 CALS PER PORTION • 34 G FAT PER PORTION • PREPARATION TIME: 15 MIN • CAN BE MADE 2 DAYS AHEAD • FREEZE-ABILITY: 1 MONTH.

VODKA-CURED SALMON WITH PINK

AND GREEN PEPPERCORNS

Place one-third of the chopped dill in a shallow, non-corrosive dish. Place one salmon fillet on top of the dill, skin-side down.

Crack the peppercorns roughly in a mortar and pestle, then sprinkle on to the salmon with the salt and sugar. Pour over the vodka and sprinkle over another third of the chopped dill. Place the other half of the salmon on top, skin-side up, and cover with the remaining chopped dill.

Cover with clingfilm and place a heavy weight on top of the fish (a foil-wrapped brick works well). Chill for up to 4 days, basting and turning twice a day.

To serve, scrape off the marinade and slice thinly across the grain of the salmon, removing the skin as you go. Serve with Dill Blinis (see recipe below).

206 CALS PER PORTION • 13 G FAT PER PORTION • PREPARATION TIME: 20 MIN. PLUS 2-4 DAYS MARINATING • CAN BE MADE 5 DAYS AHEAD • FREEZE-ABILITY: 2 MONTHS.

SERVES 8

30 g (1 oz) chopped fresh dill
1 kg (2¼ lb) middle cut fresh salmon, filleted but not skinned, pinboned
1 tbsp pink peppercorns
1 tbsp green peppercorns
30 g (1 oz) coarse sea salt
30 g (1 oz) caster sugar
2 tbsp vodka
Dill sprigs, to garnish

This version of the popular gravadlax is delicious before Christmas dinner.

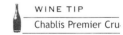 WINE TIP
Chablis Premier Cru

DILL BLINIS WITH

MUSTARD CREME FRAICHE

Process the flours, salt, baking powder, egg and milk in a liquidiser or food processor to make a batter. Stir in the dill and chill for 30 minutes.

Heat a frying pan over a medium heat until a drop of water sizzles when dropped on to the pan. Lightly grease the pan with butter, then pour in 1 tbsp of batter for each blini.

When the blinis are golden brown underneath and bubbles appear on top, turn them over and cook until the other sides are golden brown. Keep warm in a clean tea towel. If preparing the blinis in advance, layer them between sheets of greaseproof paper. Warm gently in the paper in a 100°C, 200°F, Gas ½ oven before serving.

To make the mustard crème fraîche, stir the mustard into the crème fraîche. Serve with the blinis.

59 CALS PER PORTION • 4 G FAT PER PORTION • PREPARATION TIME: 15 MIN • COOKING TIME: 25 MINUTES • CAN BE MADE UP TO 1 MONTH AHEAD • FREEZE-ABILITY: (BLINIS) 1 MONTH.

MAKES 16

55 g (2 oz) plain flour
55 g (2 oz) buckwheat flour or wholemeal flour
¼ tsp salt
½ tsp baking powder
1 medium egg, beaten
150 ml (¼ pt) milk
1 tbsp finely chopped fresh dill
Melted butter for greasing
MUSTARD CREME FRAICHE
2 tbsp wholegrain mustard
200 g (7 oz) crème fraîche

MU-SHU PORK ON LETTUCE LEAVES

MAKES ABOUT 24 PORTIONS

2 tbsp groundnut oil or vegetable oil

170 g (6 oz) pork mince

170 g (6 oz) shelled raw prawns, finely chopped

1 clove garlic, crushed

2 red chillies, de-seeded and finely diced

6 water chestnuts, finely diced

1 small carrot, peeled and diced

3 spring onions, finely diced

2 tbsp soy sauce

1 tbsp rice wine vinegar

1 tbsp brown sugar

Pinch of 5-spice powder

2 tbsp chopped fresh coriander

Salt and ground black pepper

Leaves from 3 Little Gem lettuce heads, to serve

Tapas, Chinese-style, are perfect nibbles before a Chinese feast.

WINE TIP
Alsace Pinot Blanc

Heat the oil in a sauté pan over a medium heat and cook the pork mince and prawns for about 3 minutes, or until nearly cooked through.

Add the garlic and chillies to the pan and continue to cook for about 2 minutes, or until the pork and prawns are cooked through. Remove from the pan with a slotted spoon.

Stir in all the remaining ingredients, except the lettuce leaves, and leave to cool. Store in the fridge until required.

Place spoonfuls of pork mixture on to individual lettuce leaves and serve.

33 CALS PER PORTION • 2 G FAT PER PORTION • PREPARATION TIME: 20 MIN • COOKING TIME: 15 MIN • CAN BE MADE A DAY AHEAD • FREEZE-ABILITY: CANNOT BE FROZEN.

CHAPTER FOUR

SALADS

ASPARAGUS WITH WARM LEEK

AND HAZELNUT VINAIGRETTE

SERVES 6

1 medium leek, washed and cut into
julienne strips
120 ml (4 fl oz) chicken or
vegetable stock
60 ml (2 fl oz) white wine
450 g (1 lb) asparagus tips
2 tsp fresh lemon juice
3 tbsp hazelnut oil
3 tbsp olive oil
Salt and ground black pepper
2 tbsp roughly crushed, toasted hazelnuts

Place the leek, stock and wine in a small saucepan and simmer for about 15 minutes, until the leek is tender.

Meanwhile, steam the asparagus tips for about 5 minutes, also until tender. Transfer to serving plates and keep warm.

By the time the leek is done, the cooking liquid should have reduced to 2 tbsp. If not, remove the leeks and boil the liquid to reduce it. If there's too little liquid, add water. Return the leek to the liquid.

Whisk the lemon juice and oils into the warm liquid. Season, then pour over the asparagus. Garnish with the hazelnuts and serve at room temperature. Serve with Parmesan Chive Scones (see recipe on page 179).

161 CALS PER PORTION • 15 G FAT PER PORTION • PREPARATION TIME: 10 MIN • COOKING TIME: 20 MIN •
CAN BE MADE 6 HR AHEAD • FREEZE-ABILITY: NOT ADVISABLE.

Dieters and non-dieters alike
will relish this recipe for the
best spring asparagus.

WINE TIP
Sauvignon Blanc

PORTABELLA MUSHROOM SALAD

Peel the mushrooms and discard the stems. Cut into thick wedges.

Stir the garlic into 3 tbsp of olive oil and the lemon juice. Pour over the mushrooms and leave to marinate for 1 hour.

Grill the peppers until the skins turn black, then place in a plastic bag until cool. Remove the skins and cut the peppers into thick strips.

To make the croutons, remove the crusts and cut the bread into cubes. Heat the oil until hot enough to brown a cube of bread within 30 seconds, then fry the cubes until lightly browned. Remove the croutons with a slotted spoon and place on kitchen paper. Sprinkle with salt.

To make the dressing, whisk together the vinegars and mustard. Pour in the oils whilst whisking to form a thick emulsion. Season.

Sauté the mushrooms in the remaining olive oil over a medium-high heat for about 3 minutes, until just cooked through. Add the peppers to warm for 1 minute.

In a bowl, toss the mixed salad and chicory leaves with the dressing. Divide them on to serving plates, then pile the warm mushrooms and peppers on to the salad. Serve immediately.

340 CALS PER PORTION • 28 G FAT PER PORTION • PREPARATION TIME: 15 MIN • COOKING TIME: 15 MIN • CAN BE MADE A DAY AHEAD • FREEZE-ABILITY: CANNOT BE FROZEN.

SERVES 6

450 g (1 lb) large flat mushrooms
2 cloves garlic, crushed
4 tbsp olive oil
1 tbsp fresh lemon juice
2 red peppers, de-seeded
170 g (6 oz) mixed salad leaves
2 heads of chicory, separated into leaves
CROUTONS
3 thick slices of bread
Vegetable oil for frying
Salt
DRESSING
1 tbsp balsamic vinegar
1 tbsp red wine vinegar
½ tsp whole grain mustard
2 tbsp olive oil
2 tbsp hazelnut oil
2 tbsp sunflower oil
Salt and ground black pepper

Portabella mushrooms are all the rage in America, but British field mushrooms work just as well.

WINE TIP
Beaujolais

GRILLED FENNEL AND

RED ONION SALAD

Pre-heat the grill or barbecue. Trim the feathery fronds from the fennel, reserving them for garnish. Cut the fennel bulbs and red peppers into quarters and peel and quarter the onions. Brush all the vegetables with olive oil and grill until tender and the pepper skins are blackened.

Hold the pepper quarters under cold running water and remove and discard the skins, then cut the peppers lengthways into strips.

Mix together the dressing ingredients, then pour over the warm vegetables. Chill until required. Serve warm or cold, garnished with the fennel fronds.

58 CALS PER PORTION • 3 G FAT PER PORTION •PREPARATION TIME: 10 MIN • COOKING TIME: 20 MIN • CAN BE MADE 2 DAYS AHEAD • FREEZE-ABILITY: NOT ADVISABLE.

SERVES 8

4 fennel bulbs

2 red peppers, de-seeded

8 small red onions

1 tbsp olive oil

DRESSING

2 tbsp orange juice

½ tsp Dijon mustard

1 tbsp balsamic vinegar

2 tbsp olive oil

This fresh, crunchy salad is a perfect partner to grilled meats and fish.

WINE TIP
Chianti

GRILLED VEGETABLE SALAD

WITH PARMESAN CRISPS

SERVES 6

255 g (9 oz) aubergine

255 g (9 oz) courgettes

Salt

½ tsp hot chilli flakes

1 red pepper

1 yellow pepper

2 tbsp olive oil

DRESSING

1 tbsp olive oil

1 tsp balsamic vinegar

1 tsp lemon juice

1 tsp white wine vinegar

Salt and ground black pepper

PARMESAN CRISPS

Melted butter for greasing

110 g (4 oz) Parmesan cheese,
finely grated

Lacey-thin Parmesan crisps
transform these grilled
vegetables into a
smart salad.

WINE TIP
Italian Dolcetto

Slice the aubergine and courgettes into 1 cm (½ in) thick rounds. Place the aubergine slices in a colander and sprinkle lightly with salt and chilli flakes. Leave to stand for 30 minutes.

Cut the peppers into quarters, discard the seeds, then cook, skin-side up, under a hot grill until blackened. Place the peppers in a plastic bag. When cool, peel off and discard the skins.

Rinse the aubergines, then brush them and the courgettes with the oil and cook under a hot grill until golden brown and tender.

To make the dressing, mix together all the ingredients and season to taste. Toss the vegetables in the dressing and chill until required.

Pre-heat the oven to 200°C, 400°F, Gas 6. Lightly grease a baking sheet with melted butter and heat in the oven until really hot.

To make the crisps, sprinkle Parmesan into six 7.5 cm (3 in) rounds on the hot baking sheet, using 1 tbsp of cheese for each crisp. Use a fork to spread out the cheese in a thin, even layer, then cook for 2½ minutes. Leave to set for a minute, then transfer to a wire rack until cool. Store in an airtight container until required.

To serve, pile the vegetables and dressing on to plates and arrange a Parmesan crisp on top of each pile.

179 CALS PER PORTION • 14 G FAT PER PORTION • PREPARATION TIME: 30 MIN • COOKING TIME: 25 MIN • CAN BE MADE 2 DAYS AHEAD • FREEZE-ABILITY: NOT ADVISABLE.

HOT ROCKET AND SPINACH SALAD

WITH PARMESAN CROUTONS

Remove the coarse stems from the rocket and spinach leaves. Wipe the mushrooms and trim stems, then slice thinly. Store in the fridge, covered with damp kitchen paper.

To make the croutons, pre-heat the oven to 200°C, 400°F, Gas 6. Cut the bread into 1 cm (½ in) cubes, toss in the oil and grated Parmesan and bake on a baking sheet for 8 to 10 minutes. Cool completely.

To make the dressing, cook the pancetta or bacon in a dry frying pan over a medium-high heat, stirring occasionally until the meat is lightly browned and the fat has melted. Add the garlic, ginger and chilli and cook for 1 minute, then stir in the vinegar; cook until reduced by half. Place the salad leaves in a large bowl.

Stir the remaining ingredients into the dressing and pour the hot dressing over the salad. Toss well to coat the leaves and transfer to a serving dish. Sprinkle with croutons and serve.

323 CALS PER PORTION • 36 G FAT PER PORTION • PREPARATION TIME: 15 MIN • COOKING TIME: 10 MIN •
CAN BE MADE 2 DAYS AHEAD • FREEZE-ABILITY: CANNOT BE FROZEN.

SERVES 6

55 g (2 oz) rocket leaves, washed

170 g (6 oz) baby spinach, washed

55 g (2 oz) button mushrooms

CROUTONS

55 g (2 oz) day-old coarse bread,
    crusts removed

2 tbsp olive oil

1 tbsp grated Parmesan cheese

DRESSING

200 g (7 oz) pancetta or streaky bacon,
    diced

1 clove garlic, crushed

½ tsp grated fresh ginger

1 red chilli, finely diced

60 ml (2 fl oz) red wine vinegar

1 tsp dry English mustard

1 tsp caster sugar

150 ml (¼ pt) olive oil

Rocket gives this salad a peppery twist but, if you can't find it, the spinach works just as well on its own. The croutons keep for a week in an airtight container. If you make the dressing ahead, reheat it.

WINE TIP

New Zealand
Sauvignon Blanc

CHINESE TIGER PRAWN

AND MANGETOUT SALAD

SERVES 6

SALAD

600 g (1 lb 5 oz) tiger prawns,
shelled and de-veined

1 tbsp vegetable oil

140 g (5 oz) mangetout

3 tbsp chopped fresh coriander, leaves
and tender stems only

DRESSING

90 ml (3 fl oz) rice wine vinegar

4 tsp caster sugar

2 tbsp light soy sauce

2 red chillies, de-seeded and
finely chopped

1 large clove garlic, crushed

4 spring onions, finely chopped

90 ml (3 fl oz) vegetable oil

My favourite Chinese
ingredients come together in
this recipe to make a very
special salad. To serve as a
main course, accompany with
thin rice noodles.

WINE TIP
Sauvignon Blanc

To make the dressing, heat the rice wine vinegar and caster sugar until the sugar dissolves. Stir in the other sauce ingredients. Leave to cool.

Sauté the tiger prawns in the oil over a medium-high heat for 2 to 3 minutes. They are done when they turn pink and curl up. Add the cooked tiger prawns to the dressing.

Blanch the mangetout in a large saucepan of boiling salted water for 1 minute. Drain well in a sieve, then briefly hold the sieve under cold running water to stop the mangetout cooking. Dry on kitchen paper and add to the dressing.

Stir the coriander into the dressing and chill the salad until required.

219 CALS PER PORTION • 13 G FAT PER PORTION • PREPARATION TIME: 10 MIN • COOKING TIME: 5 MIN • CAN BE MADE A DAY AHEAD • FREEZE-ABILITY: CANNOT BE FROZEN.

CHAPTER FIVE

POULTRY

TURKEY TONNATO

SERVES 6–8

1.5 kg (3 lb 5 oz) turkey breast roast
Salt and ground black pepper
Leaves from 2 sprigs of tarragon
1 tbsp capers, rinsed and chopped
2 tbsp chopped fresh flat-leaf parsley
Sprigs of flat-leaf parsley, to garnish
COURT-BOUILLON
290 ml (½ pt) dry white wine
2 stalks from sprigs of tarragon
1 tsp peppercorns
2 bay leaves
1 carrot, peeled and sliced
1 celery stick, sliced
1 small onion, sliced
SAUCE
200 g (7 oz) can of tuna, drained
255 g (9 oz) mayonnaise
5 anchovies, rinsed
1 tbsp capers, rinsed
Juice of ½ lemon
Salt and ground black pepper

This variation of the Italian vittello tonnato is perfect for summer al fresco dining.

Put the court-bouillon ingredients in a large saucepan with 1 ltr (1¾ pt) water. Bring to the boil and simmer for 20 minutes. Cool and strain.

Bone the turkey then season it and spread the tarragon leaves over it. Roll into a log and tie with string.

Put the turkey into a large saucepan and almost cover with the court-bouillon. Poach for 1½ hours then cool by standing the pan in cold water. When cold, remove the string and skin, then cut across the grain into 1 cm (½ in) slices.

Blend the sauce ingredients in a food processor, thinning with 2 tbsp of cooled poaching liquid. Season. Spread a layer of sauce in a serving dish. Add the turkey slices, coating each one with sauce. Cover with clingfilm. Refrigerate.

Sprinkle with chopped capers and parsley. Garnish with whole sprigs of parsley. Serve with crusty bread and Green Vegetable Pasta Salad (see recipe on page 119).

414 CALS PER PORTION • 27 G FAT PER PORTION • PREPARATION TIME: 20 MIN • COOKING TIME: 2 HR • CAN BE MADE A DAY AHEAD • FREEZE-ABILITY: NOT ADVISABLE.

WINE TIP
Southern
French Rosé

FRESH ROAST TURKEY WITH

A HERBY SAUSAGE STUFFING

Rinse the turkey and remove any pin feathers. Remove the giblets and neck, and discard the liver. Loosely cover the turkey and keep cool.

For the gravy, place the neck and giblets in a saucepan and cover with 1.5 ltr (2½ pt) water. Add the onion, carrot, celery, parsley, bay leaf and peppercorns. Simmer for 2 to 4 hours, skimming the surface occasionally. Discard the giblets and set the stock aside.

Meanwhile, make the stuffing. Melt the butter in a saucepan and stir in the onion and celery. Place a piece of wet greaseproof paper directly on the surface of the vegetables, then cover the pan with a lid. Cook over a low heat for 10 to 15 minutes until softened. Turn on to a plate and leave to cool.

Combine the cooled vegetables with the remaining stuffing ingredients and use some to stuff the neck cavity of the turkey. Weigh the turkey and calculate the cooking time: roast for 35 minutes per kg (15 minutes per lb). Fasten the skin flap on the underside with a skewer. Shape the remaining stuffing into 5 cm (2 in) balls. Place in a greased ovenproof dish. Chill until required.

Pre-heat the oven to 190°C, 375°F, Gas 5. Season the turkey and place on a rack in a roasting tin. Melt the butter, use to soak a piece of butter muslin and place over the breast (this avoids the need for basting). Roast the turkey for 2½ hours, or until the juice from the thickest part of the thigh runs clear. Place the stuffing balls in the oven about 1 hour before the end of cooking time.

Transfer the turkey to a warmed serving platter, remove the skewer and cover with foil to keep warm.

To finish making the gravy, add the flour to the roasting tin and cook over a medium heat until browned. Scrape the juices from the bottom, and slowly stir in the prepared stock to make a smooth gravy.

Boil the wine until reduced by half, then add to the gravy. Boil for about 15 minutes, until thickened. Sieve into a warmed gravy boat. Serve the turkey, stuffing and gravy with Candied Sweet Potatoes (see recipe on page 110) and Succotash (see recipe on page 103).

SERVES 8

4 kg (9 lb) turkey
Salt and ground black pepper
85 g (3 oz) butter

GRAVY
1 small onion, sliced
1 small carrot, peeled and sliced
2 celery sticks, sliced
2 fresh parsley stalks
1 bay leaf
1 tsp black peppercorns
30 g (1 oz) plain flour
150 ml (¼ pt) dry white wine

STUFFING
30 g (1 oz) butter
1 large onion, finely chopped
2 celery sticks, finely chopped
450 g (1 lb) good-quality sausagemeat
170 g (6 oz) fresh white breadcrumbs
15 g (½ oz) fresh parsley, chopped
1 tsp finely chopped fresh sage
Grated zest of 1 lemon
2 medium eggs, beaten
½ tsp ground mace
½ tsp ground clove
1 scant tsp salt
Freshly ground black pepper

A traditional roast turkey with all the trimmings is always a family favourite.

WINE TIP
Californian
Pinot Noir

857 CALS PER PORTION • 51 G FAT PER PORTION • PREPARATION TIME: 45 MIN • COOKING TIME: 3 HR •
STUFFING CAN BE MADE 1 MONTH AHEAD • FREEZE-ABILITY: STUFFING, 1 MONTH.

CHICKEN WITH HARISSA

AND APRICOTS

Heat the olive oil in a sauté pan. Add the chicken thighs and brown, on the skin side, over a medium to low heat. When they have browned, place the chicken thighs in an ovenproof dish large enough to hold them in a single layer and set aside.

Pour off all but 1 tbsp of fat from the sauté pan and add the onion and celery. Cover the pan with damp greaseproof paper and a lid and cook over a medium to low heat for about 15 minutes, until the vegetables are soft.

Pre-heat the oven to 180°C, 350°F, Gas 4. Remove the lid and paper from the pan, add the garlic and cook for 1 minute. Add the tomatoes, apricots, lemon juice, cinnamon and cumin. Heat gently and season with the Harissa paste and salt and pepper. Pour the mixture over the chicken, then bake in the oven for 1 hour.

Sprinkle the chicken with chopped fresh coriander and serve on a bed of mixed boiled rice, such as wild rice, Camargue red and Basmati rice. Stir in a few chopped pistachios and finely chopped fresh mint to the boiled rice for added flavour and texture. If preparing in advance, reheat at 180°C, 350°F, Gas 4 for 30 minutes.

410 CALS PER PORTION •27 G FAT PER PORTION •PREPARATION TIME: 30 MIN • COOKING TIME: 1 HR •
CAN BE MADE 2 DAYS AHEAD • FREEZE-ABILITY: 3 MONTHS AFTER COOKING.

SERVES 6

2 tbsp olive oil

12 chicken thighs with skin

225 g (8 oz) onion, chopped

2 celery stalks, chopped

2 cloves garlic, crushed

2 x 400 g (14 oz) cans of chopped
   tomatoes in tomato sauce

140 g (5 oz) dried apricots, shredded

1 tbsp lemon juice

½ tsp ground cinnamon

1 tsp ground cumin

3 tbsp Harissa paste

Salt and ground black pepper

2 tbsp chopped fresh coriander

Mixed boiled rice with pistachios and
   mint to serve

Harissa is a fiery-hot paste used in North African cooking. It is made from red chillies, garlic, cumin, coriander and mint. Rabbit makes a tasty substitute for chicken.

WINE TIP
Chilean
Pinot Noir

CHICKEN SUPREME WITH

BACON AND SAGE

SERVES 6

6 boneless chicken breasts
6 slices smoked back bacon, de-rinded
and chopped
3 tbsp ricotta cheese
3 tbsp grated mozzarella cheese
2 tbsp Parmesan cheese
1 clove garlic, crushed
1 tbsp chopped fresh parsley
Freshly ground black pepper
6 whole fresh sage leaves
Oil for brushing
150 ml (¼ pt) dry white wine
400 g (14 oz) fresh spinach
1 tsp cornflour
25 g (1 oz) butter
Fresh sage leaves, to garnish

Stuffing the chicken breasts
makes them good enough for
the smartest dinner party.

WINE TIP
Beaujolais

Pre-heat the oven to 200°C, 400°F, Gas 6. Loosen the skin at the shortest end of each chicken breast.

Process the bacon, cheeses and crushed garlic in a food processor to a smooth paste. Stir in the parsley and season with pepper.

Divide the mixture into six, then stuff it underneath the skin of the chicken breasts in an even layer and add a sage leaf to each one. Tuck the ends of the chicken skin under, then place in an ovenproof dish. Brush with oil. Pour over the dry white wine and bake for 30 minutes on the top shelf of the oven.

Wash the spinach well and remove any large stalks.

When the chicken is cooked, keep it warm by covering with foil while you cook the spinach and the sauce.

Sieve the juices from the chicken into a small saucepan. Add 1 tbsp cold water to the cornflour and stir into the juices. Boil for 1 minute to thicken.

Heat the butter in a large sauté pan over a high heat until it foams and starts to brown. Turn the spinach in the butter until it is wilted. Drain away any excess liquid, then divide the spinach between six warmed serving plates.

Top with the chicken breasts and pour over the sauce. Garnish with sage leaves and serve with Risotto Tomatoes (see recipe on page 99).

477 CALS PER PORTION • 37 G FAT PER PORTION • PREPARATION TIME: 10 MIN • COOKING TIME: 35 MIN •
CAN BE MADE A DAY AHEAD • FREEZE-ABILITY: CHICKEN STUFFED, 1 MONTH BEFORE COOKING.

THAI GREEN CURRY CHICKEN SALAD

To poach the chicken, place the chicken breast-side-up in a large pot with the onion, celery, carrot, bay leaf and seasonings. Cover with cold water and a lid. Bring to a simmer, but do not allow to boil or the meat will be tough.

Cook for approximately 1 hour until the juices run clear from the thigh when pierced with a skewer and the legs wobble in their sockets. Remove from the liquid to cool. Pull the meat from the carcass while still slightly warm. Refrigerate until required.

Blend the ingredients for the curry paste in a liquidiser until smooth.

Fry 3 tbsp of the curry paste mixture in a dry frying pan over a medium heat until the mixture splits and looks curdled. This will take about 3 minutes. The remaining curry paste mixture can be stored in a covered glass jar in the fridge for up to one week.

Add the thick coconut milk to the pan (if the milk hasn't separated in the can, only use half of it) and cook for 2 minutes. Allow the mixture to cool. It should be as thick as Greek yoghurt.

Stir the curry mixture into the mayonnaise, yoghurt and chutney, and season to taste. Pour over the chicken. Cover with clingfilm and refrigerate until required.

Serve with Thai Rice Salad (see recipe on page 118) and garnish with the coriander sprigs.

COOK'S TIP • When catering for large numbers, use boneless chicken breasts. Remove the skin, cut into bite-size pieces then bake on a roasting tin covered with foil at 180°C, 350°F, Gas 4 for about 25 minutes or until cooked through.

378 CALS PER PORTION •30 G FAT PER PORTION • PREPARATION TIME: 20 MIN • COOKING TIME: 5 MIN •
CAN BE MADE 2 DAYS AHEAD • FREEZE-ABILITY: CANNOT BE FROZEN.

SERVES 6

1.8 g (4 lb) whole chicken,
1 small onion, chopped
1 stick of celery, chopped
1 carrot, peeled and sliced
1 bay leaf
1 tsp black peppercorns
1 tsp salt
Coriander sprigs, to garnish

CURRY PASTE

4 Kenyan chillies
3 spring onions, roughly chopped
2.5 cm (1 in) piece of fresh ginger,
    peeled and chopped
1 tsp black peppercorns
3 cloves garlic
15 g (¹/₂ oz) fresh coriander, including
    the stalks
1 tsp ground lemon grass or 1 stalk fresh
Grated zest of 1 lemon
1 tsp ground cumin
1 tsp ground coriander
1 tsp salt
1 tsp shrimp paste
1 tbsp vegetable oil
1 tsp jalapeño sauce

SAUCE

400 g (14 oz) can of coconut milk
120 ml (4 fl oz) mayonnaise
150 ml (¹/₄ pt) Greek yoghurt
2 tbsp mango chutney, chopped
Salt and ground black pepper

This green curry with fresh Thai flavours makes a spicy change from Coronation Chicken.

WINE TIP
Chilean Sauvignon Blanc

This low-fat main dish is one of my favourites.

CHICKEN BREASTS WITH CARAMELISED RED ONIONS

SERVES 6

560 g (1¼ lb) red onions, thinly sliced

2 tbsp sunflower oil

6 boneless chicken breasts, skinned

Salt and ground black pepper

2 cloves garlic, crushed

2 tsp finely chopped fresh rosemary

2 tsp clear honey

Grated zest and juice of 2 oranges

1 tbsp chopped fresh parsley, to garnish

WINE TIP
Beaujolais
Villages

Put the onions and the oil in a large saucepan over a low heat, place a piece of damp greaseproof paper over them, cover with a lid and cook for about 15 minutes or until soft.

Pre-heat the oven to 180°C, 350°F, Gas 4. Place the chicken breasts in a shallow ovenproof dish and season well.

Remove the paper and lid from the onions, turn the heat to medium and continue to cook until the onions just begin to brown. Add the garlic, rosemary, honey, orange zest and juice and cook, stirring, for a further 2 minutes.

Pile the onion mixture on top of the chicken breasts, spreading it in a even layer. Bake for 40 minutes on the top shelf of the oven and serve sprinkled with parsley.

To prepare ahead, let the onion mixture cool completely before spreading it over the chicken, store in the refrigerator for up to two days and bake as above for 45 minutes.

Serve with Saffron Rice and Pasta Pilaf (see recipe on page 117).

232 CALS PER PORTION • 8 G FAT PER PORTION • PREPARATION TIME: 10 MIN • COOKING TIME: 50 MIN • CAN BE MADE 2 DAYS AHEAD • FREEZE-ABILITY: 1 MONTH AFTER COOKING.

CHICKEN BREASTS STUFFED WITH HERB MOZZARELLA WITH SUNDRIED TOMATO SALSA

Pre-heat the oven to 180°C, 350°F, Gas 4. Roast the garlic by placing the unpeeled cloves in a ramekin and baking in a moderate oven for 10 minutes until soft when pierced with a skewer.

Cut the mozzarella into 0.5cm (¼ in) slices and place in a shallow dish. Peel and crush the garlic, stir it into the oil with the herbs, then pour over the mozzarella slices.

Cut a pocket in the side of each chicken breast and season. Fill each pocket with mozzarella and secure with a cocktail stick, then turn the chicken in the leftover herb oil. Cover with clingfilm and chill overnight.

To make the salsa, pour boiling water over the sundried tomatoes and leave to soak for about 5 minutes until soft. Drain, then cut into thin slices. Mix with the chopped tomatoes, olives, oil and herbs, and chill until required. (This salsa can be made a day in advance.)

Pre-heat the grill or barbecue and cook the chicken under or over a moderate heat for 7 minutes on each side or until cooked through. Remove the cocktail sticks, garnish with basil, and serve with the salsa.

464 CALS PER PORTION • 34 G FAT PER PORTION • PREPARATION TIME: 20 MIN • COOKING TIME: 10 MIN • CAN BE MADE A DAY AHEAD • FREEZE-ABILITY: NOT ADVISABLE.

SERVES 8

2 cloves garlic
285 g (10 oz) mozzarella cheese
150 ml (¼ pt) olive oil
1 tbsp chopped fresh oregano
1 tbsp chopped fresh rosemary
8 boneless chicken breasts, skinned
Salt and ground black pepper
SALSA
100 g (3½ oz) sundried tomatoes
2 large ripe tomatoes, peeled,
    de-seeded and chopped
140 g (5 oz) pitted black olives,
    quartered
2 tbsp olive oil
2 tbsp chopped fresh parsley
1 tbsp chopped fresh oregano
Fresh basil, to garnish

This Italian-inspired chicken is perfect with Green Vegetable Pasta Salad (see recipe on page 119) and Grilled Fennel and Red Onion Salad (see recipe on page 45).

WINE TIP
Australian Cabernet Sauvignon

GUINEA FOWL WITH CIDER AND APPLES

SERVES 8

3 guinea fowl

255 g (9 oz) shallots

55 g (2 oz) pancetta or diced
streaky bacon

30 g (1 oz) butter

2 tbsp vegetable oil

6 tbsp flour, seasoned with salt
and ground black pepper

1 celery stick, diced

1 large carrot, diced

1 clove garlic, crushed

1 bay leaf

6 thyme sprigs

290 ml (½ pt) chicken stock

450 ml (16 fl oz) dry cider

1 tbsp flour plus ½ tbsp butter,
worked to a paste

60 ml (2 fl oz) double cream

FOR THE GARNISH

15 g (½ oz) butter

1 tbsp caster sugar

2 to 3 red dessert apples, cored
and cut into eighths

2 tbsp chopped fresh parsley

This fruity casserole can also
be made with pheasant.

WINE TIP
Red Bordeaux

Pre-heat the oven to 170°C, 325°F, Gas 3. Joint each guinea fowl into 8 pieces by cutting around the thigh and leg, and disjointing the leg. Cut the thigh from the drumstick and cut through the breastbone lengthways then again across at an angle through each breast (or ask a butcher to do this for you).

Peel the shallots by immersing them in boiling water for 1 minute and holding them in a sieve under the cold tap. Cut off any root hair but leave the shallots whole.

Cook the pancetta or bacon in a dry frying pan over a medium heat until lightly browned, lift out with a slotted spoon and set aside. Melt half the butter in the same frying pan with half the oil and cook the shallots over a medium heat, turning frequently, until golden. Lift out and set aside.

Coat the guinea fowl pieces with seasoned flour. Add the remaining butter and oil to the pan and brown the pieces a few at a time over a medium heat. Set aside when the pieces are all browned. Turn the heat to medium-low and cook the celery and carrot until soft. Add the garlic and cook for a further 1 minute. Transfer to a flameproof casserole.

Arrange the guinea fowl, pancetta or bacon and shallots in the casserole with the guinea fowl breasts on top. Add the bay leaf, thyme, stock and cider. Bring to simmering point, cover, transfer to the oven and cook for 1 hour.

Transfer the guinea fowl, shallots and pancetta to a serving dish and keep warm. Sieve the remaining contents of the casserole into a large saucepan and discard the herbs, celery and carrots. Whisk in the flour and butter paste. Boil for 5 minutes or until the sauce is the consistency of thick pouring cream. Stir in the cream and pour over the guinea fowl.

To make the garnish, cook the butter and sugar together in a frying pan until golden brown. Add the apple and cook on all sides until tender and golden. Garnish the serving dish with the apples and sprinkle with parsley to serve.

If peparing ahead, reheat at 180°C, 350°F, Gas 4 for 30 minutes.

1,158 CALS PER PORTION • 80 G FAT PER PORTION • PREPARATION TIME: 30 MIN • COOKING TIME: 60 MIN • CAN BE MADE A DAY AHEAD • FREEZE-ABILITY: 3 MONTHS.

SOY-BRAISED GUINEA FOWL

WITH SHIITAKE MUSHROOMS

Cover the shiitake mushrooms with 250 ml (9 fl oz) boiling water and leave for 20 to 30 minutes.

Heat the oil in a pan and brown the guinea fowl, skin-side down, over a medium heat until golden (about 8 minutes). Remove and set aside.

Cook the garlic and ginger in the pan for 1 minute, then add the Madeira or sherry, scraping the brown sediment from the bottom of the pan. Boil to reduce the liquid by half.

Return the guinea fowl pieces to the pan with the chestnuts, honey, soy sauce, stock and mushrooms with their liquid. Bring to simmering point, cover and cook over a low heat for 45 minutes. The guinea fowl is done when the juices run clear when pierced with a skewer.

Slice the guinea fowl and arrange on plates with the chestnuts and mushrooms. Bring the pan juices to the boil over a medium heat. Stir the cornflour into 2 tbsp water, then whisk into the pan juices to thicken. Boil the gravy and spoon over the guinea fowl. Serve with Sesame Rice (see recipe on page 119).

If preparing ahead, reheat at 180°C, 350°F, Gas 4 oven for 30 minutes.

530 CALS PER PORTION • 29 G FAT PER PORTION • PREPARATION TIME: 30 MIN • COOKING TIME: 50 MIN • CAN BE MADE A DAY AHEAD • FREEZE-ABILITY: 3 MONTHS.

SERVES 6

20 g (³/₄ oz) dried shiitake mushrooms

2 tbsp sunflower oil

2 guinea fowl, each jointed into 8 pieces (see opposite)

2 cloves garlic, crushed

15 g (¹/₂ oz) fresh ginger, peeled and sliced

100 ml (3¹/₂ fl oz) dry Madeira or sherry

240 g (8¹/₂ oz) vacuum-packed whole peeled chestnuts

1 tbsp honey

8 tbsp dark soy sauce

500 ml (18 fl oz) chicken stock

2 tsp cornflour

Braising produces moist, succulent meat.

WINE TIP

New Zealand
Cabernet Merlot

HONEY-GLAZED GOOSE

SERVES 8

Pre-heat the oven to 190°C, 375°F, Gas 5. Weigh the goose to establish cooking time: 35 minutes per kg (15 minutes per lb) plus 30 minutes standing time.

Pull out any pin feathers and remove lumps of fat from the body cavity. Rinse the cavity and place the apples inside.

Place the goose on a wire rack above a large roasting tin. Tie the legs together with string. Pierce all over with a thin needle, rub with salt and cook in the oven, basting occasionally. About 2 hours before the goose is cooked, drain the fat into another tin for roast potatoes. If the goose gets too dark, cover loosely with foil.

About 30 minutes before the goose is cooked, drain all but 2 tbsp of fat from the tin. Add the onion to the tin and return to oven. About 10 minutes before the goose is cooked, mix the honey, orange juice and mustard and spread the mixture over the goose. Return to the oven to glaze.

Transfer the goose to a warmed serving platter and remove the wing tips, knuckles and trussing string. Tent the goose with foil to keep warm.

To make the gravy, stir the flour into the fat in the roasting tin over a medium heat until golden. Stir in the wine, bubble for 2 minutes, then add the stock and bay leaf. Bring to the boil and simmer until thickened, adding water if needed. Season and sieve into a warmed gravy boat. Garnish the goose with watercress and kumquats and serve with the gravy and Spiced Cranberry and Kumquat Sauce (see recipe below).

5 kg (11 lb) goose (drawn weight)

2 apples, quartered

Salt

1 onion, sliced

3 tbsp clear honey

Juice of ½ orange

2 tsp English mustard

1 large bunch of watercress and whole kumquats, to garnish

GRAVY

2 tbsp flour

150 ml (¼ pt) white wine

425 ml (¾ pt) chicken stock

1 bay leaf

Salt and ground black pepper

A delectable change from the traditional turkey, goose has less meat than a similar sized turkey, so you will need a 5 kg bird to serve eight.

678 CALS PER PORTION • 42 G FAT PER PORTION • PREPARATION TIME: 20 MIN • COOKING TIME: 35 MIN PER KG • FREEZE-ABILITY: 6 MONTHS BEFORE COOKING.

WINE TIP
Australian
Cabernet Shiraz

SPICED CRANBERRY AND KUMQUAT SAUCE

SERVES 8

In a saucepan, dissolve the sugar in 4 tbsp water over a low heat.

Cut the kumquats into cranberry-sized pieces. Add the kumquats, cranberries, cloves and cinnamon to the pan and bring to the boil.

Simmer for 5 minutes, then remove from the heat and allow to cool.

Stir in the port. Cover and chill until ready to serve.

170 g (6 oz) golden caster sugar

255 g (9 oz) kumquats

255 g (9 oz) frozen cranberries, defrosted

6 whole cloves

1 cinnamon stick

4 tbsp port

105 CALS PER PORTION • 0.2 G FAT PER PORTION • PREPARATION TIME: 5 MIN • COOKING TIME: 7 MIN • CAN BE MADE 1 WEEK AHEAD • FREEZE-ABILITY: UP TO 3 MONTHS.

PHEASANT BRAISED WITH MADEIRA, PANCETTA AND BUTTERBEANS

SERVES 6–8

130 g (4½ oz) pancetta or cubed
unsmoked bacon
2 hen pheasants, jointed, or
8 pheasant breasts
2 tbsp olive oil
6 shallots, coarsely chopped
1 large carrot, diced
1 celery stick, diced
2 cloves garlic, crushed
150 ml (¼ pt) Madeira
2 x 400 g (14 oz) cans of butterbeans,
drained and rinsed
2 bay leaves
4 fresh thyme sprigs
425 ml (¾ pt) chicken stock
1 tbsp plain flour
1 tbsp softened butter
Salt and ground black pepper
Thyme sprigs, to garnish

This is the perfect way
to prepare a pheasant
of an uncertain age.

WINE TIP
Chilean
Cabernet Merlot

Pre-heat the oven to 150°C, 300°F, Gas 2. Brown the pancetta or bacon in a large ovenproof casserole over a medium heat. Remove with a slotted spoon and set aside.

Brown the pheasant in the pancetta fat. Remove from the casserole and set aside.

Add the oil to the casserole and cook the shallots, carrot and celery until lightly browned. Add the garlic and cook for a further 30 seconds.

Pour in the Madeira and allow to bubble until reduced by half.

Place the butterbeans, bay leaves and thyme in the casserole, followed by the pancetta and pheasant. Pour over the stock and bring to a simmer. Cover and place in the oven for 1 hour, or until the pheasant is tender.

To serve, remove the pheasant, butterbeans and vegetables from the casserole using a slotted spoon and place in a warmed serving dish. Remove and discard the bay leaves and thyme stalks. Mix the flour and butter to form a paste, then whisk into the sauce. Leave to boil for 2 to 3 minutes until thick and glossy. Season and pour over the pheasant. Garnish with thyme sprigs.

If prepared in advance, reheat at 180°C, 350°F, Gas 4 for 30 minutes.

500 CALS PER PORTION • 24 G FAT PER PORTION •PREPARATION TIME: 20 MIN • COOKING TIME: 1½ HR • CAN BE MADE A DAY AHEAD • FREEZE-ABILITY: 1 MONTH AFTER COOKING.

LEMON AND HERB-CRUSTED POUSSIN

Pre-heat the oven to 200°C, 400°F, Gas 6. Grate the zest from the lemon and set aside. Cut the remaining lemon into chunks, squeeze the juice into the poussins then push the lemon pieces into the body cavities. Place the poussins in a large roasting tin and set aside.

Mix the garlic, herbs and reserved lemon zest into the butter, and spread over the breasts and legs of the poussins. Sprinkle with salt and pepper, then pat the breadcrumbs on to the butter-smeared birds.

Roast in the oven for 30 minutes for single poussins; 45 minutes for double poussins. The birds are cooked when the juices run clear when a thigh is pierced at its thickest point with a skewer. Leave the poussins to stand for 10 minutes.

Double poussins should be divided into two by cutting either side of the backbone and dividing the breast from one end to the other with a pair of sturdy scissors. Garnish with flat-leaf parsley and serve with Glazed Spring Vegetables (see recipe on page 102).

472 CALS PER PORTION • 34 G FAT PER PORTION • PREPARATION TIME: 10 MIN • COOKING TIME: 45 MIN •
CAN BE MADE A DAY AHEAD • FREEZE-ABILITY: NOT ADVISABLE.

SERVES 6

1 lemon

6 single or 3 double poussins

1 clove garlic, crushed

2 tbsp chopped fresh parsley

2 tsp chopped fresh thyme

55 g (2 oz) butter, softened

Salt and ground black pepper

3 tbsp fresh white breadcrumbs

Flat-leaf parsley, to garnish

Use single or double poussins for this special spring dish. The poussins can be spread with the herb butter a day in advance then kept in the fridge.

WINE TIP
Beaujolais

This stunning presentation is easy to achieve and is a mouthwatering, yet simple way to serve duck.

FIVE-SPICE DUCK BREASTS
WITH PAK CHOI AND MANGETOUT

SERVES 8

8 x 225 g (8 oz) Gressingham duck breasts
2 tbsp groundnut oil for frying
MARINADE
1 tbsp sesame oil
2 tbsp Chinese 5-spice powder
2 tsp chilli powder
3 tbsp soy sauce
Whole red chillies, to garnish

WINE TIP
New Zealand
Pinot Noir

Remove the skin from the duck breasts and discard.

Mix together all the marinade ingredients and use to coat the duck. Chill for 1 hour or overnight.

Pre-heat the oven to 200°C, 400°F, Gas 6. Heat enough groundnut oil in a sauté pan to just cover the bottom of the pan. Fry the duck breasts over a medium heat for 2 minutes on each side to brown.

Place the duck breasts on a baking sheet and cook in the top of the oven for 10 minutes (the meat should still be pink). Remove and leave to stand for 10 minutes.

Slice the duck, arrange on plates and garnish with whole red chillies. Serve with Stir-fried Pak Choi and Mangetout (see recipe on page 101) and Thai Noodles (see recipe on page 115).

270 CALS PER PORTION • 13 G FAT PER PORTION • PREPARATION TIME: 20 MIN • COOKING TIME: 10 MIN •
DUCK CAN BE MARINATED A DAY AHEAD • FREEZE-ABILITY: MARINATED DUCK, 3 MONTHS.

CHAPTER SIX

MEAT

LEG OF LAMB BRAISED WITH
SPRING VEGETABLES

SERVES 6

2 kg (4 lb 4 oz) whole leg of lamb

Salt and ground black pepper

1 clove garlic, crushed

55 g (2 oz) butter, softened

150 ml (¼ pt) dry white wine

290 ml (½ pt) brown stock

750 g (1 lb 10 oz) new potatoes, scrubbed

340 g (12 oz) baby carrots, peeled

340 g (12 oz) petits pois

1 tbsp flour

4 tbsp double cream

2 tbsp chopped fresh mint

This is my family's favourite way to have a joint of lamb. Start preparation at least 2 hours before you want to eat.

WINE TIP
Red Bordeaux

Cut away any skin and membrane from the lamb to expose the meat and cover with black pepper. Mix the garlic into the butter, spread it over the lamb and leave to stand at room temperature for 30 minutes while the oven pre-heats to 180°C, 350°F, Gas 4.

Heat a large, flameproof casserole over a medium heat and brown the lamb. Pour in the wine and stock and allow to bubble for 2 minutes. Cover with a lid and transfer to the oven for 1½ hours.

After 30 minutes add the potatoes; 30 minutes later, add the carrots and petit pois.

When the lamb is cooked and the vegetables are tender, transfer to a large platter and cover with foil. Stir the flour into the cream and, over a medium heat, whisk this into the hot stock in the casserole. Boil for about 5 minutes until syrupy, season, stir in the mint and pour over the lamb before serving.

The lamb can be kept warm in a 100°C, 200°F, Gas ½ oven for up to an hour.

691 CALS PER PORTION • 41 G FAT PER PORTION • PREPARATION TIME: 25 MIN • COOKING TIME: 1 HR 35 MIN • FREEZE-ABILITY: UNCOOKED LAMB CAN BE FROZEN FOR 6 MONTHS.

CROWN ROAST OF LAMB WITH SAFFRON COUSCOUS AND APRICOT STUFFING

Pre-heat the oven to 200°C, 400°F, Gas 6. To make the gravy, place the lamb trimmings, onion and carrot in a large roasting tin and coat with the oil. Cook in the hottest part of the oven, stirring occasionally, for 30 minutes until well browned.

Drain the fat from the lamb trimmings and vegetables, reserving 2 tbsp of the fat. Transfer the lamb and vegetables to a large pan with the bay leaf, peppercorns, parsley stalks and 1 ltr (1¾ pt) cold water. Bring to the boil, reduce heat and simmer, skimming occasionally, for 2 hours. Sieve and reserve 570 ml (1 pt) of the stock.

In a separate pan, stir the flour and reserved fat over a low heat until the flour is browned. Remove from the heat and slowly stir in the reserved stock. Return to the heat, add the wine and simmer for 20 minutes until syrupy. Sieve and chill until required.

For the couscous stuffing, bring the stock to the boil, then add the saffron and salt. Remove from the heat and leave to stand for 5 minutes.

Place the couscous in a bowl and pour over the hot stock and the oil. Stir with a fork to break up any lumps. Allow to stand for 10 minutes. Add the chopped dried apricots and leave to cool. When cool, stir in the spring onions, parsley and pine nuts.

Place the crown roasts of lamb in two roasting tins or shallow ovenproof dishes and fill each centre with the couscous stuffing. Cover the stuffing and the ends of the lamb bones with foil. Push thin slices of garlic into the spaces between the cutlets and roast for 35 to 40 minutes until the meat is cooked. Remove from the oven and leave to stand for 10 minutes.

To serve, transfer the crowns of lamb to the plate, using a fish slice to prevent the stuffing from falling out. Warm the red wine gravy and serve with the lamb.

872 CALS PER PORTION • 65 G FAT PER PORTION • PREPARATION TIME: 30 MIN FOR THE SAUCE PLUS 2 HR SIMMERING TIME. 10 15 MIN FOR THE STUFFING. 20 MIN FOR THE LAMB • COOKING TIME: 40 MIN PLUS 10 MIN STANDING • STUFFING CAN BE MADE A DAY AHEAD • FREEZE-ABILITY: MEAT CAN BE FROZEN FOR 6 MONTHS.

SERVES 8

4 x 8-bone racks of lamb, tied into
   2 crown roasts
2 cloves garlic, peeled and thinly sliced
RED WINE GRAVY
Trimmings from the lamb
1 small onion, cut into quarters
1 small carrot, peeled and cut
   into large chunks
1 tbsp olive oil
1 bay leaf
½ tsp peppercorns
3 parsley stalks
2 tbsp flour
150 ml (¼ pt) red wine, reduced by half
COUSCOUS STUFFING
425 ml (¾ pt) chicken or vegetable stock
½ tsp saffron strands
½ tsp salt
255 g (9 oz) uncooked couscous
3 tbsp olive oil
85 g (3 oz) dried apricots, chopped
1 bunch of spring onions, finely chopped
2 tbsp chopped fresh parsley
100 g (3½ oz) pine nuts, toasted

A crown roast is a spectacular centrepiece for a special meal. The trimmings are full of flavour and perfect for making the red wine gravy.

WINE TIP
Australian Cabernet
Shiraz

LAMB FILLETS IN FILO PASTRY

SERVES 6

4 best end necks of lamb weighing about
500 g (1 lb 2 oz) each, chined

A little oil for frying and brushing

6 large spinach leaves

12 filo pastry sheets (about 340 g)

1 egg, beaten

2 tbsp sesame seeds, toasted

MARINADE

3 tbsp balsamic vinegar

1 tbsp clear honey

1 tbsp finely chopped fresh rosemary

Mint sprigs, to garnish

The oriental marinade adds lots of flavour to the lamb without adding too many calories.

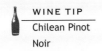

WINE TIP

Chilean Pinot
Noir

Cut around the eye of the meat to remove the fillet from the bones. Cut each fillet in half crossways to make six equal-sized pieces.

Combine the marinade ingredients in a plastic bag. Add the lamb pieces to the bag and chill for at least 1 hour or up to 24 hours.

Heat enough oil in a sauté pan to coat the bottom of the pan and fry the lamb pieces until lightly browned on all sides. Transfer to a plate to cool.

Blanch the spinach leaves by dipping them in boiling water until wilted. Drain on kitchen paper.

Wrap a spinach leaf around each piece of lamb. Brush the filo sheets with a little oil and wrap each piece of lamb in 4 layers of pastry. If not cooking immediately, cover with clingfilm and set aside until required.

Pre-heat the oven to 225°C, 425°F, Gas 6. Brush each filo parcel with egg and sprinkle with sesame seeds. Place on a baking sheet and cook in the oven for 10 to 12 minutes. Garnish with mint sprigs and serve with Tomato, Mint and Courgette Salsa (see recipe below).

345 CALS PER PORTION • 16 G FAT PER PORTION • PREPARATION TIME: 35 MIN • MARINATING TIME: AT LEAST 1 HR • COOKING TIME: 12 MIN • CAN BE MADE A DAY AHEAD • FREEZE-ABILITY: 1 MONTH.

TOMATO, MINT AND COURGETTE SALSA

SERVES 6

4 tomatoes

225 g (8 oz) small courgettes, finely diced

2 tbsp chopped fresh mint

1 shallot, finely diced

4 tsp balsamic vinegar

4 tbsp olive oil

Peel the tomatoes by immersing them in boiling water for about 10 seconds then plunging them into cold water. Peel the skins from the tomatoes – they should come away easily.

De-seed the tomatoes and cut into dice. Combine with the remaining ingredients and chill until required.

84 CALS PER PORTION • 8 G FAT PER PORTION • PREPARATION TIME: 15 MIN • COOKING TIME: NONE • CAN BE MADE 6 HR AHEAD • FREEZE-ABILITY: CANNOT BE FROZEN.

MOROCCAN SPICED LOIN OF LAMB

SERVES 6

4 best end necks of lamb, weighing about
500 g (1 lb 2 oz) each, chined

Juice of ½ lemon

Salt and ground black pepper

4 tbsp plain yoghurt

1 clove garlic, crushed

SPICE MIX

1 tbsp cumin seeds

1 tbsp coriander seeds

1 cinnamon stick, crumbled

1 tbsp fennel seeds

Seeds from 2 cardamom pods

Parsley sprigs, to garnish

Harissa paste, to serve

For the spice mix, place the cumin, coriander, cinnamon, fennel and cardamom in a small frying pan and toast over a low heat for 2 minutes. Remove from the heat and leave to cool.

Grind the spices in a pestle and mortar, then stir into the yoghurt, along with the garlic.

Cut around the eye of the meat to remove the fillet from the bones. Squeeze over the lemon juice. Season well, coat with the spiced yoghurt and chill for at least 2 hours or overnight.

Pre-heat the oven to 220°C, 425°F, Gas 7, or heat the barbecue to high. Roast the lamb for 12 to 14 minutes, or barbecue for 4 minutes on each side. Leave to stand for 15 minutes before carving into thin slices. Arrange the lamb on a bed of Lemon Couscous (see recipe on page 120), garnish with parsley and serve with ready-made harissa paste, if desired.

242 CALS PER PORTION • 13 G FAT PER PORTION • PREPARATION TIME: 15 MIN • COOKING TIME: 8-14 MIN • CAN BE MADE A DAY AHEAD • FREEZE-ABILITY: 1 MONTH.

If you're short of time, ask your butcher to bone out the eye of the meat from the lamb. Beef fillet or duck breasts could be substituted for the lamb – adjust the cooking time to suit the thickness of the meat.

WINE TIP
Australian
Shiraz

PORK FILLET STUFFED WITH

TOULOUSE SAUSAGES AND PRUNES

Pre-heat the oven to 190°C, 375°F, Gas 5. Trim any membrane from the pork fillets, then cut through the meat lengthways to open each fillet out into a rectangular shape. Flatten it to 1 cm (½ in) thick by batting it with a meat tenderiser or the bottom of a heavy saucepan.

Cut the prunes in half, and soak them in thè brandy.

Discard any tough stalks from the spinach, then cook it in a small amount of boiling water until it just wilts. Drain well in a sieve. Squeeze dry when cool and chop roughly.

Remove the sausagemeat from the sausage casings. Combine the sausagemeat with the spinach and breadcrumbs, and season with the salt and pepper.

Lay the pork fillets out flat with the cut sides facing uppermost and season. Spread the stuffing over each fillet, then lay the prunes end-to-end down the centre. Roll the fillets so prunes are encased in stuffing. Tie each fillet with string in 4 or 5 places.

Heat the oil in a heavy-based casserole or sauté pan. Brown the fillets well on all sides.

Add the shallots, carrot and tomato to the pan with the fillets, then cover and place in the oven for 40 minutes. Test if the meat is cooked by inserting a metal skewer into the middle of the pork for 10 seconds. It should feel hot when removed and any juices which escape should be clear, not pink.

When the fillets are cooked, place on a serving dish and tent with foil to keep warm.

Place the pan in which the pork was cooked over a medium-high heat. Add the wine and let it bubble until 2 tbsp remain, then add the stock and reduce it to half its original volume. Make the flour and butter into a paste and whisk this into the sauce. Season, then pass the sauce through a sieve and discard the vegetables.

To serve, remove the string from the fillets and slice them into 2 cm (¾ in) slices. Surround with the sauce and serve with Pommes Boulangere (see recipe on page 107).

SERVES 6–8

900 g (2 lb) pork fillet (2 fillets)
110 g (4 oz) pitted prunes
2 tbsp brandy
200g (7 oz) fresh spinach
400 g (14 oz) Toulouse sausages
55 g (2 oz) white breadcrumbs
½ tsp salt
Freshly ground black pepper
1 tbsp olive oil
4 shallots, roughly chopped
1 small carrot, peeled and cut
    into 1 cm (³⁄₈ in) dice
1 small tomato, roughly chopped
150 ml (¼ pt) red wine
425 ml (¾ pt) chicken stock
2 tsp plain flour
2 tsp butter, softened
Shredded green cabbage, to serve

Toulouse sausages, fragrant with garlic are well worth seeking out for this recipe.

WINE TIP
Southern French
Grenache

606 CALS PER PORTION • 35 G FAT PER PORTION • PREPARATION TIME: 30 MIN • COOKING TIME: 50 MIN •
CAN BE MADE 2 DAYS AHEAD • FREEZE-ABILITY: 1 MONTH BEFORE COOKING.

CHEESE-CRUSTED PORK CHOPS

Place 1 tbsp of the oil in a small saucepan and stir in the onion. Place a piece of damp greaseproof paper on the onion and cover with a lid. Cook for 15 minutes over a low heat until the onion is very soft.

Place the remaining oil in a sauté pan over a medium heat. Season the chops and sauté on both sides until browned. Remove from the pan and place in a single layer in an ovenproof dish.

Pre-heat the oven to 200°C, 400°F, Gas 6. Combine the Madeira and stock and pour into the hot sauté pan. Scrape over the bottom of the pan to remove the sediment and bring the sauce to the boil. Boil for 5 minutes, then remove the pan from the heat and set aside.

Mix together the breadcrumbs, cheese and herbs, then stir in 2 tbsp of the Madeira sauce. Pat the mixture on to the top of each chop in an even layer and cook in the oven for 30 minutes, or until the chops are cooked through and toppings are browned and crusty.

Mix the cornflour with 1 tbsp water, stir into the remaining Madeira sauce and bring to the boil. Garnish the chops with parsley and serve with the sauce and Individual Pommes Boulangere (see recipe on page 107).

337 CALS PER PORTION • 26 G FAT PER PORTION • PREPARATION TIME: 30 MIN • COOKING TIME: 30 MIN • CAN BE MADE A DAY AHEAD • FREEZE-ABILITY: 6 MONTHS.

SERVES 6

2 tbsp sunflower oil

1 small onion, finely chopped

Salt and ground black pepper

6 boneless pork loin chops

2 tbsp Madeira

290 ml (½ pt) chicken stock

55 g (2 oz) fresh wholewheat breadcrumbs

55 g (2 oz) Gruyère or strong
   Cheddar cheese, grated

1 tbsp chopped fresh thyme

1 tbsp chopped fresh parsley

2 tsp cornflour

Parsley sprigs, to garnish

A crusty cheese and herb topping keeps the pork chops succulent and tender.

WINE TIP
French Syrah

PORK FILLET WITH WHOLEGRAIN

MUSTARD SAUCE

SERVES 6

3 tbsp sunflower oil

30 g (1 oz) butter

2 large onions, thinly sliced

675 g (1½ lb) pork fillet

Salt and ground black pepper

60 ml (2 fl oz) white wine

200 ml (7 fl oz) chicken stock

4 tbsp wholegrain mustard

2 tsp cornflour

6 tbsp crème fraîche

3 tbsp chopped fresh coriander

Steamed courgettes, to serve

Make this pork with piquant sauce in advance and reheat gently in a sauté pan. Add the coriander just before serving, otherwise it will lose its colour and flavour.

WINE TIP
Chilean Merlot

Place the oil and butter in a sauté pan over a low heat. When the butter has melted, add the onion and stir until coated. Place a piece of damp greaseproof paper on the onions and cover with a lid. Cook over a low heat for about 15 minutes until softened.

Trim any membrane from the pork and cut the meat across the grain into 2.5 cm (1 in) thick medallions. Season.

Using a slotted spoon, remove the onions from the pan and set aside. Increase the heat under the pan to medium-high and quickly brown the pork on both sides. Do not add too much meat to the pan at once or it will steam and not brown. Remove from the pan and set aside.

Add the wine to the pan and scrape in the meat sediment from the bottom. Stir in the stock and mustard, then return the meat and onions to the pan. Cover, reduce the heat and simmer for about 20 minutes until the pork is cooked through.

Using a slotted spoon, remove the meat and onions from the pan and place in a warmed serving dish.

Stir the cornflour into the crème fraîche and whisk the mixture into the cooking liquid in the pan. Bubble until thickened. Stir in the coriander and pour the sauce over the pork. Serve with thinly sliced steamed courgettes.

381 CALS PER PORTION • 27 G FAT PER PORTION • PREPARATION TIME: 20 MIN • COOKING TIME: 40 MIN • CAN BE MADE A DAY AHEAD • FREEZE-ABILITY: 6 MONTHS.

PORK FILLET WITH WILD

MUSHROOMS EN CROUTE

Trim any fat and membrane from the pork fillets and split them in half lengthways. Combine the marinade ingredients in a large plastic bag or non-corrosive bowl and marinate the pork for 4 hours or overnight in the fridge.

Pre-heat the oven to 200°C, 400°F, Gas 6. Pour 150 ml (5 fl oz) boiling water over the porcini mushrooms in a small bowl or heatproof cup and leave to stand for 20 minutes. Drain and chop finely, then mix with the other mushrooms.

Roll half the puff pastry very thinly to an oblong about 20 x 40 cm (8 x 16 in) to make a base for the pork. Prick all over with a fork, chill until firm, then bake in the oven for 15 minutes until lightly browned. Cool on a wire rack.

Lift the pork from the marinade and dry on kitchen paper. Heat the oil in a large sauté pan over a medium to high heat and brown the pork well on all sides. Transfer to a roasting tin and bake for 15 minutes or until cooked through. Cool. Meanwhile boil the marinade to reduce by half. Add to the meat juices.

Melt the butter in a large sauté pan over a medium heat and soften the shallots or spring onions. Add the mushrooms and cook for 5 minutes or until the liquid has evaporated. Stir in the breadcrumbs and parsley and leave to cool.

Wash the spinach leaves. Blanch the leaves by dipping them into first boiling then cold water. Dry on kitchen paper and remove any large stalks.

Put the cooked pastry on a baking sheet, sprinkle with semolina, cover with a few spinach leaves and trim off excess pastry. Layer the pork and mushroom stuffing alternately then cover with the rest of the spinach leaves.

Roll the remaining pastry thinly and cover the pork, trimming and tucking the edges underneath the pastry base. Decorate with raw pastry trimmings. Beat the egg yolks with 1 tbsp cold water and paint over the pastry to glaze. Chill overnight.

To make the sauce, stir the flour into the meat juices in the roasting tin and cook, stirring, until it browns. Stir in the stock and strained marinade and allow to bubble until it has a syrupy consistency. Cool until required.

Pre-heat the oven to 200°C, 400°F, Gas 6. Bake on the top shelf for 40 minutes, until the pastry is well browned. Serve with the reheated sauce.

SERVES 6

1 kg (2 lb 4 oz) pork fillet
40 g (1½ oz) dried porcini mushrooms
255 g (9 oz) fresh closed-cap mushrooms, finely chopped
MARINADE
290 ml (½ pt) red wine
2 tsp Worcestershire sauce
1 tsp dry English mustard powder
1 clove garlic, crushed
5 cm (2 in) piece of fresh ginger, grated
675 g (1½ lb) puff pastry
2 tbsp cooking oil
30 g (1 oz) butter
4 tbsp finely chopped shallots or spring onions
4 tbsp fresh white breadcrumbs
4 tbsp chopped fresh parsley
2 tsp flour
150 ml (¼ pt) brown stock
12 large fresh spinach leaves
2 tbsp semolina
2 egg yolks to glaze pastry

An impressive main course that includes fresh and dried mushrooms. Make it a day ahead and then bake just before the meal.

WINE TIP
Chilean Pinot Noir

912 CALS PER PORTION • 51 G FAT PER PORTION • PREPARATION TIME: 30 MIN PLUS MARINATING AND CHILLING TIME • COOKING TIME: 55 MIN • CAN BE MADE A DAY AHEAD • FREEZE-ABILITY: 1 MONTH BEFORE COOKING.

FILLET OF BEEF EN CROUTE

SERVES 8

1.6 kg (3 lb 7 oz) trimmed beef fillet
from the thick end
Freshly ground black pepper
Worcestershire sauce
675 g (1½ lb) puff pastry
2 tbsp oil
150 ml (¼ pt) dry Madeira
225 g (8 oz) brown cap mushrooms,
chopped
1 tsp chopped fresh thyme
1 egg, beaten
SAUCE
1 onion, coarsely chopped
1 tbsp diced carrots
1 tbsp diced celery
1 tbsp oil
1 tbsp plain flour
900 ml (1½ pt) beef stock
Watercress, to garnish

This impressive dish can
be made a day in advance
and kept in the fridge
before baking.

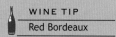

WINE TIP
Red Bordeaux

Pre-heat the oven to 220°C, 425°F, Gas 7. Tie the beef with string at 2.5 cm (1 in) intervals. Season with black pepper and Worcestershire sauce.

Roll out one-third of the pastry thinly, so it's about 5 cm (2 in) larger than the fillet on all sides. Place on a baking sheet and prick all over with a fork. Bake for 15 to 20 minutes until golden and cooked through, then place on a wire rack to cool.

Heat 1 tbsp of the oil over a medium heat in a sauté pan or roasting tin large enough to hold the beef. Brown the beef well, then place on a wire rack in another roasting tin and roast for 20 minutes.

Meanwhile, pour the Madeira into the hot pan. Allow it to bubble until halved in quantity, then set aside for the sauce. Put the remaining oil in a sauté pan and cook the mushrooms until their juices evaporate. Stir in the thyme and season. Allow to cool.

Place the cooked pastry on a baking sheet and spread the cooked mushrooms over it. Remove the string from the beef and place the beef on top of the mushrooms. Trim the pastry to the size of the beef.

Roll out the remaining pastry and cover the beef completely. Cut the excess pastry from the corners and reserve for decoration.

Brush the edges of the pastry with the beaten egg, then tuck them under the beef with a palette knife. Glaze the pastry, decorate with the trimmings, glaze the decorations and reserve the remaining egg. Chill overnight, or until very firm.

To make the sauce, brown the vegetables in the oil. Stir in the flour and cook until deep brown. Remove from the heat, slowly stir in the stock, then add the reduced Madeira. Return to the heat and simmer for at least 30 minutes, until syrupy. Pass through a sieve.

To cook the beef, pre-heat the oven to 220°C, 425°F, Gas 7. Glaze the pastry with the reserved egg, then bake for 25 minutes for rare beef, 35 minutes for medium, or 45 minutes for well done. Cover the pastry with greaseproof paper after about 20 minutes to stop it becoming too brown.

Leave to stand for 15 to 20 minutes before carving. Garnish with watercress and serve hot or cold with the sauce, reheated if necessary, and Pommes Dauphinois (see recipe on page 111).

693 CALS PER PORTION • 37 G FAT PER PORTION • PREPARATION TIME: 50 MIN • COOKING TIME: 25–45 MIN • CAN BE MADE A DAY AHEAD • FREEZE-ABILITY: CANNOT BE FROZEN.

CURRIED PORK FILLET

AND RED PEPPER SAUTE

SERVES 6

700 g (1½ lb) pork fillet

3 tbsp sunflower oil

1 large red pepper, de-seeded
and thinly sliced

2 shallots, finely chopped

1 red chilli, finely chopped (optional)

2 tsp grated root ginger

1 tsp whole cumin seeds, crushed

1 clove garlic, crushed

290 ml (½ pt) chicken stock

400 ml (14 fl oz) coconut milk

Salt and ground black pepper

3 tbsp chopped fresh coriander

This quick-to-make stir-fry
is even better the next
day when the spices have
permeated the meat.

WINE TIP
Californian Zinfandel

Trim any membrane from the pork, then cut the meat at an angle into strips 1 cm (½ in) thick and 4 cm (1½ in) long. Heat 2 tbsp of oil in a sauté pan over a medium heat and brown a few pieces at a time, transferring them to a dish as they brown.

When all the pork is browned, turn the heat to low, add the remaining oil and cook the red pepper and shallots until they begin to soften. Add the chilli, if using, the ginger, cumin seeds and garlic and cook for a further 1 minute before adding the chicken stock and coconut milk.

Scrape the bottom of the pan and mix into the sauce. Return the pork and any juices to the pan and simmer for about 15 minutes or until the pork is firm. The dish can be cooled, refrigerated or frozen at this point.

To serve, transfer the reheated pork and peppers to a serving dish and keep warm. Boil the sauce to the thickness of single cream, season, stir in the coriander and pour over pork. Serve with boiled rice.

382 CALS PER PORTION • 22 G FAT PER PORTION • PREPARATION TIME: 10 MIN • COOKING TIME: 30 MIN • CAN BE MADE 2 DAYS AHEAD • FREEZE-ABILITY: 1 MONTH.

BEEF AND RED ONION KEBABS

ON ROSEMARY SKEWERS

Place the steak in a large plastic bag. Combine the ingredients for the marinade and pour over the steak. Chill for at least 2 hours or overnight.

Wash the courgettes, top and tail them, then cut into 2½ cm (1 in) pieces. Place in the plastic bag with the steak and leave to marinate for 1 hour.

Peel the onions, separate into layers then cut into 2.5 cm (1in) squares.

Remove all but the top 5 cm (2 in) of leaves from the rosemary stems and soak in cold water for 10 minutes.

Use a skewer to pierce the meat and vegetables, then thread the steak, onions and courgettes alternately on to the rosemary skewers and chill until required.

Pre-heat the grill or barbecue. Cook the kebabs under a hot grill or on the barbecue for 3 to 4 minutes per side. Serve with Red Onion Focaccia bread (see recipe on page 182).

399 CALS PER PORTION • 20 G FAT PER PORTION • PREPARATION TIME: 20 MIN • COOKING TIME: 6–8 MIN • CAN BE MADE A DAY AHEAD • FREEZE-ABILITY: BEEF IN THE MARINADE, 3 MONTHS.

SERVES 6

675 g (1½ lb) sirloin steak, cut
   into 2½ cm (1 in) cubes
3 medium courgettes
2 large red onions
12 x 25 cm (10 in) long stems of rosemary
MARINADE
6 tbsp Tamari soy sauce
6 tbsp dry sherry
2 tbsp vegetable oil
1 tsp freshly grated root ginger
1 clove garlic, crushed
1 tsp caster sugar
½ tsp wasabi powder

This dish is ideal for a summer barbecue. Marinate the beef for 24 hours before cooking for extra flavour.

WINE TIP
Australian Cabernet
Merlot

CARBONADE OF BEEF

SERVES 6 – 8

1.35 kg (3 lb) chuck steak

2 tbsp oil

450 g (1 lb) onions, thinly sliced

2 cloves garlic, crushed

1 tbsp soft brown sugar

1 tbsp plain flour

425 ml (¾ pt) brown ale

425 ml (¾ pt) brown stock

1 tsp chopped fresh thyme

1 bay leaf

2 tsp red wine vinegar

Salt and ground black pepper

8 French bread slices

8 tbsp wholegrain mustard

This classic Belgian casserole
uses ale to enrich the sauce
and tenderise the meat.

WINE TIP
Chilean Merlot

Sauté the onions in a little oil in a saucepan for 20 minutes. Cover with a damp piece of greaseproof paper and a lid. Cook in a saucepan over a low heat for 15 minutes.

Pre-heat the oven to 150°C, 300°F, Gas 2. Cut the beef across the grain into 7 x 5 cm (3 x 2½ in) steaks.

Heat enough oil to just cover the base of a large frying pan and brown the beef over a medium heat, a few pieces at a time, pouring in a little water between batches to remove any brown colour from the base of the pan. Reserve the liquid. Place the beef in an ovenproof casserole dish.

Remove the lid and paper from the onions. Add the garlic and sugar, and cook for 1 minute. Stir in the flour, then continue to cook until lightly browned. Add the ale, stock and reserved liquid. Simmer, stirring, for 2 minutes. Add the herbs, vinegar and seasoning.

Pour the stock mixture over the meat in the casserole, cover and cook in the oven for 2½ hours. (If making ahead, cook the casserole to this point. Reheat at 180°C, 350°F, Gas 4, for 30 minutes.)

To serve, increase the oven temperature to 190°C, 375°F, Gas 5. Remove the bay leaf from the casserole and discard. Spread the bread slices with the mustard and place, mustard-side up, on top of the casserole. Cook, uncovered, for 15 minutes. Serve with Glazed Carrots with Orange and Nutmeg (see recipe on page 103) and new potatoes.

505 CALS PER PORTION • 23 G FAT PER PORTION • PREPARATION TIME: 30 MIN • COOKING TIME: 2 HR 30 MIN • CAN BE MADE 2 DAYS AHEAD • FREEZE-ABILITY: 6 MONTHS.

VENISON CASSEROLE WITH

SOUR CHERRIES AND PORT

SERVES 6

900 g (2 lb) venison steaks

6 tbsp sunflower oil

425 ml (¾ pt) beef stock or water

110 g (4 oz) dried sour cherries

3 tbsp port

Salt and ground black pepper

3 tbsp chopped fresh parsley, to garnish

MARINADE

425 ml (¾ pt) orange juice

240 ml (8 fl oz) full-bodied red wine

175 g (6 oz) onions, finely sliced

8 juniper berries, roughly crushed

2 cloves garlic, sliced

2 tbsp sunflower oil

1 bay leaf

Make this fruity casserole
a day or two ahead to allow
the flavours to mellow.

WINE TIP
New Zealand
Merlot

Remove any fat and membrane from the venison and cut the meat into 7 x 5 cm (3 x 2 in) pieces. Combine the marinade ingredients in a bowl, add the venison and refrigerate overnight.

Pre-heat the oven to 150°C, 300°F, Gas 2. Remove the venison from the marinade and pat dry with kitchen paper. Strain the marinade, and reserve the liquid and flavouring ingredients separately.

Brown the venison in batches on both sides over a medium heat, using enough oil to cover the bottom of the pan. Between batches, swirl a little marinade in the pan. Add the liquid to a large flameproof casserole along with the meat.

Brown the onions from the marinade in the remaining oil, and add them to the casserole with stock or water and any remaining marinade. Bring to simmering point, cover and cook in the oven for 2 hours. Meanwhile, soak the cherries in the port.

Transfer the meat to a warmed serving dish. Remove the bay leaf from the casserole then liquidise the remaining contents. Add the cherries and port to this sauce, simmer for 5 minutes, then season and pour over the meat. Garnish with parsley and serve with Garlic and Olive Oil Mashed Potatoes (see recipe on page 109).

440 CALS PER PORTION • 19 G FAT PER PORTION • PREPARATION TIME: 40 MIN PLUS MARINATING OVERNIGHT • COOKING TIME: 2 HOURS • CAN BE MADE 2 DAYS AHEAD • FREEZE-ABILITY: 3 MONTHS.

VEAL NOISETTES WITH PEPPERS

AND RED ONION MARMALADE

Pre-heat the grill to high. Quarter the peppers, discarding the cores and seeds. Grill skin-side up until blackened, then place in a plastic bag to cool. (The steam will loosen the skins.) Discard the skins and cut the peppers in 1 cm (½ in) strips. Set aside.

To make the marmalade, heat the oil in a pan and stir in the onions. Place a piece of damp greaseproof paper on the surface of the onions, cover with a lid and cook over a low heat for 15 minutes. Remove the lid and paper, and continue to cook for 15 minutes. Stir in the tomatoes, vinegar, sugar and rosemary, and cook over a low heat for 20 minutes. Season well. Leave to cool, then chill.

Brush a griddle or frying pan with 1 tbsp of oil and fry the peppers briefly on both sides. Keep warm.

Sprinkle the veal with the vinegar, then with the rosemary and season. Brush the griddle with the remaining oil and cook the veal over a medium-high heat for 5 minutes on each side. Loosely cover with foil and leave to stand for 10 minutes.

Warm the marmalade and serve with the veal and peppers.

310 CALS PER PORTION • 11 G FAT PER PORTION • PREPARATION TIME: 45 MIN • COOKING TIME: 45 MIN • PEPPERS AND MARMALADE CAN BE PREPARED 2 DAYS AHEAD • FREEZE-ABILITY: NOT ADVISABLE.

SERVES 8

2 red peppers

2 yellow peppers

2 orange peppers

3 tbsp olive oil

8 x 170 g (6 oz) veal noisettes
from the fillet or loin

2 tbsp balsamic vinegar

2 tbsp chopped fresh rosemary

Salt and ground black pepper

ONION MARMALADE

2 tbsp olive oil

2 red onions, thinly sliced

400 g (14 oz) can of chopped tomatoes

2 tbsp balsamic vinegar

2 tbsp brown sugar

1 tbsp finely chopped fresh rosemary

Salt and ground black pepper

In this quick and easy recipe, you can grill the peppers and make the marmalade in advance. The veal takes just 10 minutes to cook.

WINE TIP
Italian Sangiovese

OVERLEAF •VEAL NOISETTES WITH PEPPERS AND ONION MARMALADE

CHAPTER SEVEN

FISH

SEAFOOD LASAGNE

SERVES 8

500 g (1 lb 2 oz) frozen leaf spinach

570 ml (1 pt) milk

4 tbsp white wine

Slice of onion,

1 bay leaf,

Black peppercorns

310g (11 oz) salmon fillet

255 g (9 oz) monkfish fillet

110 g (4 oz) onion, finely chopped

55 g (2 oz) butter

2 cloves garlic, crushed

450 g (1 lb) cottage cheese

110 g (4 oz) mozzarella, diced

4 tbsp freshly grated Parmesan cheese

1 tbsp chopped fresh parsley

1 medium egg, beaten

Salt and ground black pepper

55 g (2 oz) plain flour

150 ml (¼ pt) single cream

255 g (9 oz) cooked, peeled prawns

2 tbsp chopped fresh dill

1 tbsp lemon juice

200 g (7 oz) no pre-cook lasagne

This is a great dish to assemble ahead and freeze for a supper party. Defrost for 24 hours in the fridge and bake as directed.

WINE TIP
Californian
Chardonnay

Pre-heat the oven to 180°C, 350°F, Gas 4. Put the spinach into a sieve to defrost. When it has thawed, pick out any large stems and discard. Squeeze the leaves dry.

Heat the milk with the wine, onion slice, bay leaf and a few peppercorns in a large saucepan. Put the fish into the infused milk, cover with a piece of dampened grease-proof paper and cook gently for about 5 minutes until the fish flakes easily. Remove the fish from the milk with a slotted spoon and flake into a bowl. Sieve the milk and reserve.

Soften the onion in the butter over a low heat, add the garlic and cook for a further 1 minute. Using a slotted spoon, place the onion and garlic into a bowl to cool. Reserve the butter in the saucepan. Add the cottage cheese, mozzarella, 2 tbsp of Parmesan, the parsley and egg. Stir to combine and season.

Stir the flour into the butter left in the pan, cook for 30 seconds, then lift off the heat and gradually stir in the reserved milk. When the mixture is smooth, bring it to the boil over a medium heat. Simmer for 2 minutes then stir in the cream, remove from the heat and season. Allow to cool.

Reserve 420 ml (14 fl oz) of the sauce for the top of the lasagne. Spread a little of the rest over the base of a 33 x 23 x 5 cm (13 x 9 x 2 in) lasagne dish, stir 2 tbsp into the spinach and the remainder into the flaked fish along with the prawns, dill and lemon juice. Adjust the seasoning.

Fill the dish with a quarter of the lasagne, then a layer of spinach, lasagne, the cheese mixture, lasagne, the fish and a final layer of lasagne. Coat with the reserved sauce and sprinkle with the remaining Parmesan.

Bake for 45 minutes until bubbling and golden brown on top. Serve with salad and crusty bread.

529 CALS PER PORTION • 27 G FAT PER PORTION • PREPARATION TIME: 40 MIN • COOKING TIME: 45 MIN • CAN BE MADE A DAY AHEAD • FREEZE-ABILITY: 1 MONTH.

JAMBALAYA

Pre-heat the oven to 180°C, 350°F, Gas 4 and then put a baking dish in to warm.

Fry the diced gammon and slices of chorizo in the oil in a large frying pan over a medium heat until lightly browned, then add the onion, celery and green pepper. Turn the heat down to low, cover the pan with a lid and cook for about 15 minutes until all the vegetables have softened.

Remove the lid, turn the heat up to high, and add the chicken, stirring regularly until lightly coloured. Turn the heat down to medium, add the garlic and cook for a further 1 minute, then stir in all the remaining ingredients except the mussels, petits pois and prawns. Bring to a simmer then turn into the warmed dish, cover with foil and bake for 30 minutes. If making ahead prepare to this point. Cool then refrigerate.

Meanwhile, prepare the mussels, if you are using them. Tip them into a sink of cold water, discarding any that feel too heavy for their size as they are probably full of sand, any chipped or broken ones and any that are open. Scrub them, scraping off any barnacles and pulling away their beards.

After 30 minutes, stir the petits pois and prawns plus the mussels, if using, into the baking dish, cover with foil and bake for a further 15 minutes.

Taste and adjust the seasoning, sprinkle with coriander and serve.

343 CALS PER PORTION • 12 G FAT PER PORTION • PREPARATION TIME: 20 MIN • COOKING TIME: 45 MIN • CAN BE MADE A DAY AHEAD • FREEZE-ABILITY: NOT ADVISABLE.

SERVES 6-8

85 g (3 oz) gammon steak, diced

85 g (3 oz) chorizo, sliced
   0.5 cm (¼ in) thick

2 tbsp sunflower oil

1 large Spanish onion, chopped

2 celery sticks, chopped

1 small green pepper, de-seeded
   and chopped

2 boneless chicken thighs cut into
   2 cm (1 in) cubes

1 clove garlic, crushed

400 g (14 oz) can chopped tomatoes
   in juice

1 bay leaf

340 g (12 oz) American long-grain rice

1 tsp freeze-dried oregano

1 tsp salt

Freshly ground black pepper

½ tsp ground cumin

Pinch of cayenne

570 ml (1 pt) chicken stock

500 g (1 lb 2 oz) mussels, optional

170 g (6 oz) frozen petits pois, defrosted

130 g (4½ oz) peeled prawns

15 g (½ oz) fresh coriander, chopped

Jambalaya comes from the Creole kitchens of Louisiana. It's quick to make and a good one-pot meal for a supper party.

WINE TIP
Australian
Chardonnay

SOY MARINATED WHOLE SALMON

Remove the guts and gills from the fish and cut off the fins.

Place the ingredients for the court-bouillon in a large saucepan with 1 ltr (1¾ pt) water and simmer for 20 minutes.

Pre-heat the oven to 200°C, 400°F, Gas 6. Line a roasting tin with foil and place the fish on the foil. Strain the warm court-bouillon over the fish and cover the tin with foil.

Bake the fish in the oven for 5 minutes per 450 g (1 lb) then remove from the oven and leave to stand for 10 minutes.

To make spring onion curls, cut 7 cm (3 in) pieces of spring onion. Cut each end finely lengthways leaving 1 cm (½ in) in the centre uncut. Place in iced water for 30 minutes.

To make the marinade, warm all the ingredients in a saucepan.

Remove the fish from the court-bouillon and carefully strip off the skin from the upper side. Flip the fish over on to a lipped serving dish, then remove skin from the other side of the fish.

Pour the marinade over the fish and allow the fish to stand for 10 minutes if serving warm. If serving cold, leave the fish to cool then place in the fridge until required. Garnish with curled spring onions and serve with Coriander Cracked Wheat Salad (see recipe on page 116) and Chinese Marinated Vegetable Salad (see recipe on page 104).

SERVES 8

1.8 kg (4 lb) whole fish, such as
  salmon or sea bass
½ bunch of spring onions, curled, to
  garnish
COURT-BOUILLON
150 ml (¼ pt) dry white wine
1 bay leaf
1 celery stick, chopped
A few fresh parsley and coriander stalks
1 tsp black peppercorns
Slice of onion
MARINADE
8 tbsp good-quality light soy sauce
½ bunch of spring onions, chopped
1 tsp freshly grated ginger

A simple and delicious
way to prepare a
whole fish.

WINE TIP
German Riesling

257 CALS PER PORTION • 16 G FAT PER PORTION • PREPARATION TIME: 40 MIN • COOKING TIME: ABOUT 30 MIN • CAN BE MADE 2 DAYS AHEAD • FREEZE-ABILITY: CANNOT BE FROZEN.

ROASTED RED MULLET WITH

BROAD BEAN PUREE AND SAFFRON

AND PEPPER SAUCE

SERVES 6

6 x 140 g (5 oz) red mullet, red snapper
or Jamaican red tilapia fillets

3 tbsp olive oil

6 cloves garlic

Salt and ground black pepper

450 g (1 lb) baby new potatoes, cooked

BROAD BEAN PUREE

1 kg (2¼ lb) shelled broad beans,
skins removed

30 g (1 oz) butter

6 tbsp crème fraîche

Fresh lemon juice to taste

Salt and ground black pepper

SAFFRON AND PEPPER SAUCE

150 ml (¼ pt) fish stock

Pinch of saffron strands

150 ml (¼ pt) double cream

1 tsp pink peppercorns

Salt and ground black pepper

Chervil sprigs, to garnish

Remove any bones from the fish fillets. Place in the fridge.

Pre-heat the oven to 200°C, 400°F, Gas 6. To make the broad bean purée, cook the beans in boiling salted water for about 10 minutes, or until tender. Drain and refresh under cold running water, then purée in a food processor with the butter. Beat in the crème fraîche and season with the lemon juice and salt and pepper. Keep warm.

To make the saffron and pepper sauce, bring the fish stock to a simmer, then add the saffron. Remove from the heat. Leave to infuse for 10 minutes, then sieve the stock into the cream. Add the peppercorns, then simmer until the sauce is the consistency of single cream. Season and keep warm.

Place the olive oil and the garlic cloves in a roasting tin and cook in the oven for 10 minutes.

Season the fish fillets and place, skin-side down, in a single layer in the hot roasting tin. Return to the oven for 5 to 10 minutes until the fish is opaque.

To serve, place the broad bean purée in the centre of six warmed plates and top with a fish fillet. Surround with the sauce and serve with new potatoes. Garnish with a roast garlic clove and chervil.

594 CALS PER PORTION • 37 G FAT PER PORTION • PREPARATION TIME: 10 MIN • COOKING TIME: 20 MIN •
PUREE AND SAUCE CAN BE MADE A DAY AHEAD • FREEZE-ABILITY: NOT ADVISABLE.

This recipe combines striking colours and flavours and can be prepared quickly.

WINE TIP

New Zealand
Pinot Noir

RED SNAPPER BAKED WITH HERBS

WITH LIME GARLIC SAUCE

To make the marinade, mix all the ingredients in a bowl and set aside. With a very sharp knife, make horizontal slashes at 2.5 cm (1 in) intervals on both sides of the fish. Cut through the skin and nearly down to the bone.

Brush the marinade on to the fish working it into the slashes and inside the fish. Wrap with clingfilm and place in the fridge to marinate for at least 1 hour or overnight.

To cook in the oven, pre-heat the oven to 200°C, 400°F, Gas 6. Lightly oil a piece of foil large enough to wrap the fish. Place the fish on the foil. Boil the wine or vermouth in a saucepan until reduced by half, then stir in the herbs and pour over the fish. Fold the edges of the foil together to form a loose parcel. Place in a roasting tin.

Bake the fish for 10 minutes per 450 g (1 lb) or until cooked through. The fish is cooked when the flesh is just firm and opaque. Its eyes will have turned white and the dorsal fin (along the backbone) can be pulled out easily. Open up the foil parcel and place it on a serving plate. Garnish the fish with herb sprigs and serve.

To cook on a barbecue, start the barbecue so it is hot when you are ready to use it. Brush the barbecue rack with oil, then cook the fish for 1 minute a side for a small fish or 2 minutes a side for a large one. Wrap the fish in foil with the wine or vermouth, as instructed above.

Place the parcel on the barbecue and cook for 10 minutes per 450 g (1 lb). Halfway through the cooking time, turn the fish over. Open up the foil and place it on a serving plate with herb sprigs.

232 CALS PER PORTION • 16 G FAT PER PORTION • PREPARATION TIME: 20 MIN • COOKING TIME: 40 MIN • CANNOT BE MADE AHEAD • FREEZE-ABILITY: NOT ADVISABLE.

LIME GARLIC SAUCE

Combine all the ingredients and store in the fridge until required.

60 CALS PER PORTION • 6 G FAT PER PORTION • PREPARATION TIME: 5 MIN • COOKING TIME: NONE • CAN BE MADE 1 DAY AHEAD • FREEZE-ABILITY: CANNOT BE FROZEN.

SERVES 8

1.8 kg (4 lb) whole red snapper, mullet or sea bass

Olive or sunflower oil (for oiling foil, brushing barbecue rack

400 ml (14 fl oz) dry white wine or dry vermouth

8 tbsp chopped mixed fresh herbs such as oregano, chives, parsley, tarragon

Herb sprigs, to garnish

MARINADE

100 ml (3½ fl oz) olive or sunflower oil

3 tbsp fresh lime juice

1 tbsp ground tumeric

3 cloves garlic, crushed

Salt and ground black pepper

This is a spectacular way to prepare a whole fish, particularly when cooking on a barbecue. As a guide, plan on a serving of 255 g (9 oz) to 340 g (12 oz) fish per person. Ask your fishmonger to clean and scale the fish.

WINE TIP
Californian
Fume Blanc

4 tbsp mayonnaise

4 tbsp yoghurt

Grated zest and juice of 1 lime

1 clove garlic, crushed

Salt to taste

SALMON FILLETS WITH

A PISTACHIO CRUST

Discard any bones from the salmon fillets and place the fish in a shallow ovenproof dish. Brush the top of the fillets with the egg, and season. Combine the pistachio nuts and breadcrumbs in a bowl, then press on top of the salmon.

If preparing ahead, cover with clingfilm and place in the fridge.

Pre-heat the oven to 200°C, 400°F, Gas 6. Bake the salmon on the top shelf of the oven for 12 to 15 minutes or until opaque and firm to the touch. Serve immediately with Garlic and Olive Oil Mashed Potatoes (see recipe on page 109) and Sweetcorn and Red Pepper Salsa (see recipe below).

419 CALS PER PORTION • 23 G FAT PER PORTION • PREPARATION TIME: 5 MIN • COOKING TIME: 15 MIN • CAN BE MADE A DAY AHEAD • FREEZE-ABILITY: 3 MONTHS.

SERVES 6

6 x 110 g (4 oz) salmon fillets, skinned

1 egg, beaten

Salt and ground black pepper

55 g (2 oz) shelled pistachio nuts,
    roughly crushed

4 tbsp fresh white breadcrumbs, sieved

WINE TIP
Alsace Pinot
Gris

SWEETCORN AND RED PEPPER SALSA

Place the oil in a sauté pan, add the chillies and red pepper and cook over a low heat for 3 minutes. Set aside to cool. Stir in the remaining ingredients and chill until needed.

160 CALS PER PORTION • 12 G FAT PER PORTION • PREPARATION TIME: 10 MIN • COOKING TIME: 3 MIN • CAN BE MADE 2 DAYS AHEAD • FREEZE-ABILITY: NOT ADVISABLE.

SERVES 6

6 tbsp olive oil

2 green chillies, de-seeded and
    finely diced

1 red pepper, de-seeded and diced

340 g (12 oz) canned sweetcorn, drained

Juice of 1 lime

15 g (½ oz) fresh coriander leaves and
    tender stems, chopped

1 tbsp finely chopped fresh chives

Salsas are a great way to add texture and spice to a dish.

PRAWN AND AVOCADO PASTA

SERVES 6

450 g (1 lb) linguine pasta
2 ripe avocados
Juice of 1 lime
2 tbsp olive oil
675 g (1½ lb) raw tiger prawns,
peeled and de-veined
2 cloves garlic, crushed
2 green chillis, de-seeded and diced
300 ml (½ pt) crème fraîche
2 tbsp snipped fresh chives
Salt and ground black pepper
4 tbsp chopped fresh coriander
6 tbsp freshly grated Parmesan cheese

Cook the pasta in a large pan of boiling salted water.

Meanwhile, cut the avocados into chunks and toss with the lime juice to prevent them from going brown. Set aside.

Heat the oil in a sauté pan over a medium heat. Add the prawns and cook, stirring continuously, for about 3 minutes, or until they turn pink and are firm to touch.

Add the garlic and chillis to the prawns in the pan and cook for 30 seconds. Add the avocado and lime juice, crème fraîche and chives and heat through. Season to taste.

Drain the cooked pasta and toss with the sauce. Pile into bowls and sprinkle with the coriander and Parmesan. Serve with crusty bread.

384 CALS PER PORTION • 20 G FAT PER PORTION • PREPARATION TIME: 10 MIN • COOKING TIME: 10 MIN • CANNOT BE MADE AHEAD • FREEZE-ABILITY: NOT ADVISABLE.

This recipe combines prawns, avocados and pasta for a luxurious supper dish.

WINE TIP
Spanish/French
Dry Rosé

MONKFISH WRAPPED IN

PARMA HAM WITH SAGE

Remove the bones from the monkfish and discard, then pare away the grey membrane and discard. Cut the monkfish into 8 pieces, place in a shallow dish and sprinkle with salt and pepper. Coat with the olive oil and lemon juice, then sprinkle with the chopped sage.

Wrap each piece of monkfish in a slice of Parma ham, then wrap in non-PVC clingfilm. Chill until required.

Fill a sauté pan large enough to hold the monkfish in a single layer with 8 cm (3 in) water and bring to the boil. Place the wrapped monkfish in the water, turn the heat down to simmering and poach the monkfish for 7 to 8 minutes until firm when pressed with your finger.

Discard the clingfilm, transfer the monkfish to serving plates and garnish with parsley. Serve with Warm Broad Bean Salad (see recipe on page 101) and Sautéed New Potatoes (see recipe on page 108).

158 CALS PER PORTION • 5 G FAT PER PORTION • PREPARATION TIME: 20 MIN • COOKING TIME: 10 MIN • CAN BE MADE A DAY AHEAD • FREEZE-ABILITY: 3 MONTHS.

SERVES 8

1.35 kg (3 lb) monkfish tail
Salt and ground black pepper
2 tbsp olive oil
2 tsp lemon juice
2 tbsp chopped fresh sage
8 Parma ham slices
Fresh flat-leaf parsley, to garnish

This simple-to-prepare dish is an impressive and tasty way to serve this firm, white fish.

WINE TIP
Australian
Chardonnay

This is a fish and chips dish for adults. For a tasty alternative, substitute any firm white fish, such as swordfish, for the sea bass.

SWEET CHILLI SEA BASS

SERVES 6

6 x 110 g (4 oz) sea bass fillets
MARINADE
2 tbsp muscovado sugar
2 tbsp white wine vinegar
1 clove garlic, crushed
1 red chilli, de-seeded and chopped
1 cm (¹/₂ in) piece of fresh ginger, peeled and grated
15 g (¹/₂ oz) fresh coriander
Zest and juice of ¹/₂ lemon
1 tbsp soy sauce
Fresh coriander sprigs, to garnish

Check the fish for bones and remove.

To make the marinade, combine the sugar and vinegar in a small saucepan and heat slowly until the sugar dissolves. Remove from the heat and leave to cool. Add the remaining marinade ingredients, then liquidise to a smooth paste. Leave in a lidded jar in the fridge until required.

About 2 hours before cooking the sea bass, place the fish in a single layer in a shallow dish and pour the marinade over the top. Chill until required.

Pre-heat the grill to hot. Remove the fish from the marinade, discard the marinade and cook for 3 minutes on each side, or until it turns opaque and flakes easily. Garnish with coriander and serve with Spicy Potato Wedges (see recipe on page 107) and Green Chilli Sauce (see recipe below).

125 CALS PER PORTION • 3 G FAT PER PORTION • PREPARATION TIME: 15 MIN • COOKING TIME: 10 MIN • CAN BE MADE 1 WEEK AHEAD • FREEZE-ABILITY: MARINATED 2 MONTHS.

SERVES 6

GREEN CHILLI SAUCE

2 green chillies
30 g (1 oz) fresh coriander
55 g (2 oz) pine nuts, toasted
2 cloves garlic, crushed
30 g (1 oz) Parmesan cheese
6 tbsp olive oil
Salt and ground black pepper

Carefully slit the chillies and discard the seeds. Put the chillies, coriander, pine nuts and garlic in a processor and blend well.

Add the Parmesan to the processor and, with the motor still running, add the olive oil in a thin, steady stream until well blended. Season to taste. Thin the sauce with a little water, if necessary.

183 CALS PER PORTION • 17 G FAT PER PORTION • PREPARATION TIME: 10 MIN • COOKING TIME: 10 MIN • CAN BE MADE 1 WEEK AHEAD • FREEZE-ABILITY: NOT ADVISABLE.

CHAPTER EIGHT

VEGETABLES

BASIC VEGETABLE PREPARATION

Always buy the best quality vegetables you can afford. Look for vegetables that are in season, firm and unblemished as they that will have the greatest nutritional value and taste the best.

Buy only enough vegetables to last for a couple of days. If they are stored for a long period they lose their nutritional value so, it is better to use ones that have been frozen at their peak of ripeness and freshness than ones that have been stored, either by the shop or yourself, for a long time.

As vegetables don't take kindly to being prepared in advance it is best to prepare them as close as possible to the time of cooking. Don't soak them in water as the vitamins will disappear. For the same reason, don't add bicarbonate of soda to the cooking water.

Boil vegetables that grow above the ground in enough boiling, salted water to just cover them. Keep the lid of the pan off. When they are just cooked, drain them in a sieve then pass the sieve under cold running water. This is called refreshing and is done to stop the vegetables cooking and set in the colour. It will not make them cold if done quickly. Season and serve immediately.

If vegetables grow below the ground, place them in enough cold, salted water to just cover them and simmer them with the lid on, until cooked. Drain in a sieve or colander. Season and serve immediately.

Vegetables can also be steamed, stir-fried and baked. Last-minute preparation is difficult when entertaining. Don't choose vegetables that will be impossible to cope with immediately before serving. Take into account the quantity you will need to cook for the number of people you are catering for, and the capacity of your pans and kitchen. Remember a good salad can often take the place of hot, cooked vegetables.

When I am entertaining, I wash/top and tail/peel/slice vegetables as required before my guests arrive. To boil them I set a large pan of salted water on to simmer when the guests arrive. When I am clearing the table of the first-course plates I tip the vegetables in the water. They are done by the time I need to serve them.

If I am entertaining large numbers of people, or if the vegetables take more than 10 minutes to cook, I blanch (half cook) and refresh them until they are cold before my guests arrive. I heat the water as described above, then tip the nearly cooked vegetables into the water to finish cooking when I clear the table of the first-course plates. Although this is not ideal from a nutritional standpoint, it works perfectly.

RISOTTO TOMATOES

Melt the butter in a large sauté pan with the olive oil and gently cook the onion over a low heat until soft.

Heat the stock to boiling point, then turn down the heat and keep it simmering.

Add the rice to the onion in the pan and cook, stirring, until the rice turns opaque – about 2 minutes.

Add 100 ml (3½ fl oz) of hot vegetable stock to the rice, stirring continuously over a medium-low heat. When the stock has evaporated, repeat the procedure until the rice is just cooked through, yet still has some 'bite'. The risotto should be creamy, not runny. This will take about 20 minutes.

Stir in all but 2 tbsp of Parmesan and all the parsley, then turn the risotto on to a plate to cool. Additional stock should be stirred into the risotto as it cools to maintain the creamy texture.

Cut a thin slice from the tops of the tomatoes and scoop out the insides with a teaspoon. Turn the tomato shells upside down on kitchen paper to drain.

When the risotto is cool, pile it into the tomato shells and then place them in an ovenproof serving dish.

Mix together the remaining Parmesan and the breadcrumbs, then sprinkle over the tops of the tomatoes. The tomatoes can be covered with clingfilm and stored in the fridge until ready to bake.

To bake, pre-heat the oven to 200°C, 400°F, Gas 6. Place the tomatoes on the top shelf for 20 minutes until the tops turn golden brown. Serve.

303 CALS PER PORTION • 12 G FAT PER PORTION • PREPARATION TIME: 5 MIN • COOKING TIME: 40 MIN • CAN BE MADE A DAY AHEAD • FREEZE-ABILITY: CANNOT BE FROZEN.

SERVES 6/MAKES 12

30 g (1 oz) butter

2 tbsp olive oil

1 small onion, finely chopped

1.2 ltr (2 pt) well-seasoned vegetable stock

225 g (8 oz) Arborio rice

55 g (2 oz) grated Parmesan cheese

2 tbsp chopped fresh parsley

12 firm, ripe tomatoes

2 tbsp fresh white breadcrumbs

Piling the risotto inside the tomatoes is a clever way to prepare risotto in advance and keeps it moist.

STIR-FRIED PAK CHOI

AND MANGETOUT

Wash the pak choi well, as the base can be very gritty.

Heat the oil in a wok or frying pan. Stir in the garlic and ginger and cook for 30 seconds. Add the mangetout and cook, stirring, for 2 minutes. Add the pak choi and cook, stirring, for a further 2 minutes.

Serve immediately.

71 CALS PER PORTION • 2.5 G FAT PER PORTION • PREPARATION TIME: 10 MIN • COOKING TIME: 5 MIN • CANNOT BE MADE AHEAD • FREEZE-ABILITY: CANNOT BE FROZEN.

SERVES 8

2 tbsp groundnut oil

1 clove garlic, crushed

1 tsp grated fresh ginger

450 g (1 lb) mangetout, topped and tailed

675 g (1½ lb) pak choi, torn into bite-size pieces

Pak choi is a type of Chinese cabbage.

WARM BROAD BEAN SALAD

Shell the beans and cook in boiling, salted water for 4 minutes until tender. Drain and refresh under cold running water. Discard the grey skins and set aside.

Heat the olive oil in a large sauté pan over a medium heat and cook the celery, leeks and green pepper for 5 minutes. Stir in the garlic and cook for a further 1 minute.

Remove from the heat, add the lemon juice, then stir in the broad beans. Sprinkle over the chopped parsley and season. Serve warm.

158 CALS PER PORTION • 5 G FAT PER PORTION • PREPARATION TIME: 20 MIN • COOKING TIME: 10 MIN • CAN BE MADE A DAY AHEAD • FREEZE-ABILITY: CANNOT BE FROZEN.

SERVES 8

1.35 kg (3 lb) young broad beans

90 ml (3 fl oz) olive oil

3 celery sticks, thinly sliced

2 leeks, thinly sliced

1 green pepper, de-seeded and diced

1 clove garlic, peeled and crushed

1 tbsp lemon juice

2 tbsp chopped fresh parsley

Salt and ground black pepper

Make the most of baby broad beans with this full-of-flavour salad.

WILD MUSHROOM BREAD PUDDING

SERVES 8
AS AN ACCOMPANIMENT

15 g (½ oz) dried porcini mushrooms
55 g (2 oz) butter
1 small onion, finely chopped
1 celery stick, finely chopped
110 g (4 oz) shiitake mushrooms
110 g (4 oz) button mushrooms
Butter for greasing
140 g (5 oz) good-quality,
slightly stale white bread
1 tsp chopped fresh thyme
1 tbsp chopped fresh parsley
55 g (2 oz) walnuts, chopped
4 medium eggs, beaten
290 ml (½ pt) single cream
290 ml (½ pt) milk
Salt and ground black pepper

This dish is perfect either as a stuffing with roast poultry or as a vegetarian main course.

Place the porcini mushrooms in a small bowl and pour over 100 ml (3½ fl oz) boiling water. Set aside.

Melt the butter in a saucepan, then add the onion and celery. Place a piece of damp greaseproof paper on the vegetables and cover with a lid. Cook over a low heat for 15 minutes or until soft. Remove the lid and paper.

Slice the fresh mushrooms then add to the pan. Cook for 5 minutes until tender then set aside to cool.

Butter a 1 ltr (1¼ pt) flan dish. Discard the crusts from the bread, then cut into 1 cm (½ in) cubes. Place in the flan dish and sprinkle with the herbs and walnuts.

Combine the eggs, cream and milk. Remove the porcini from the water and add to the vegetables. Add the porcini water to the cream mixture, taking care to leave any grit in the bowl. Season well.

Stir the vegetables into the bread, then pour the egg mixture over the top. Leave to stand for 30 minutes or cover with clingfilm and chill for up to 24 hours.

Pre-heat the oven to 150°C, 300°F, Gas 2. Bake on the middle shelf for 30 minutes or until the eggs are set. Brown under the grill for 2 minutes, if desired.

165 CALS PER PORTION • 13 G FAT PER PORTION • PREPARATION TIME: 30 MIN • COOKING TIME: 30 MIN • CAN BE MADE A DAY AHEAD • FREEZE-ABILITY: CANNOT BE FROZEN.

GLAZED SPRING VEGETABLES

SERVES 6

675 g (1½ lb) baby new potatoes,
scraped
450 g (1 lb) baby carrots, scraped
3 leeks, washed and cut into chunks
30 g (1 oz) butter
1 tbsp clear honey
Salt and ground black pepper
2 tbsp chopped fresh parsley

To prepare the vegetables in advance, steam or boil them until just cooked. To steam, the potatoes will take about 15 minutes, the carrots 10 minutes and the leeks 5 minutes. Cool.

To glaze the vegetables, pre-heat the oven to 200°C, 400°F, Gas 5. Melt the butter in a roasting tin, then stir in the honey. Toss the vegetables in the honey mixture and cook in the oven for 10 minutes to heat through. Season with salt and pepper and sprinkle with chopped parsley to serve.

165 CALS PER PORTION • 5 G FAT PER PORTION • PREPARATION TIME: 5 MIN • COOKING TIME: 25 MIN • CAN BE MADE A DAY AHEAD • FREEZE-ABILITY: NOT ADVISABLE.

SUCCOTASH

Bring a large saucepan of salted water to the boil. Add the sweetcorn and beans and simmer for 3 to 4 minutes.

Meanwhile, heat the oil in a small saucepan over a medium heat and cook the red pepper for 2 minutes.

Drain the sweetcorn and broad beans and add to the pepper. Stir in the butter and season. Turn into a warmed dish and serve immediately.

159 CALS PER PORTION • 7 G FAT PER PORTION • PREPARATION TIME: 25 MIN • COOKING TIME: 5 MIN • CAN BE MADE A DAY AHEAD • FREEZE-ABILITY: NOT ADVISABLE.

SERVES 8

500 g (1 lb 2 oz) frozen sweetcorn, defrosted

750 g (1 lb 10 oz) frozen broad beans, defrosted and shelled

1 tbsp oil

1 red pepper, de-seeded and diced

30 g (1 oz) butter

Salt and ground black pepper

Succotash is an American-Indian word meaning 'boiled corn'. Prepare the vegetables a day in advance and reheat just before serving.

GLAZED CARROTS WITH ORANGE AND NUTMEG

Place all the ingredients except the parsley in a saucepan and bring to boil. Reduce the heat to a simmer, cover the pan and cook for 6 minutes until the carrots are just tender.

Remove the lid, increase the heat and reduce liquid to a syrupy glaze. Serve garnished with chopped parsley.

75 CALS PER PORTION • 4 G FAT PER PORTION • PREPARATION TIME: 5 MIN • COOKING TIME: 10 MIN • CAN BE MADE A DAY AHEAD • FREEZE-ABILITY: NOT ADVISABLE.

SERVES 8

675 g (1½ lb) carrots, peeled and sliced

290 ml (½ pt) orange juice

1 tsp caster sugar

30 g (1 oz) butter

1 tsp grated nutmeg

Salt and ground black pepper

Chopped fresh parsley, to garnish

Adding orange and spice to carrots makes them an extra-special accompaniment for roast meats and casseroles.

CHINESE MARINATED

VEGETABLE SALAD

SERVES 8

POACHING SYRUP
1 tsp salt
4 tbsp caster sugar
4 tbsp rice wine vinegar

SALAD
285 g (10 oz) mangetout, topped
and tailed
300 g (10 oz) baby sweetcorn
2 red peppers, thinly sliced

DRESSING
2 tbsp sesame seeds
2 tbsp caster sugar
4 tbsp rice wine vinegar
2 tbsp sesame oil
2 tbsp soy sauce

Place the poaching syrup ingredients in a saucepan large enough to cook the vegetables, and make the liquid up to 570 ml (1 pt) with water. Bring to the boil and simmer for 5 minutes.

Cook each type of vegetable separately in the poaching liquid until it begins to soften. Remove from the pan with a slotted spoon, then place in a sieve and pass under cold running water to stop the cooking process.

To make the dressing, fry the sesame seeds in a small saucepan over a medium heat until lightly browned. Combine with the remaining ingredients and pour over the vegetables. Place in the fridge until needed, up to 24 hours in advance.

100 CALS PER PORTION • 5 G FAT PER PORTION • PREPARATION TIME: 10 MIN • COOKING TIME: 10 MIN • CAN BE MADE A DAY AHEAD • FREEZE-ABILITY: CANNOT BE FROZEN.

Blanching the vegetables in a light syrup until they are tender but crisp allows the salad to be prepared the day before.

CHAPTER NINE

POTATOES

TYPES OF POTATOES AND

RECOMMENDED USES

England is blessed with an enormous variety of potatoes – which can be confusing for the new cook. Very simply, potatoes can be divided into two categories depending on their texture: waxy or floury.

Small, new potatoes are usually waxy. The skin of a new potato should scrape away easily. They hold their shape when boiled and are particularly good served hot, with butter or olive oil and sea salt, or cold in salads. The most prized new potato is the Jersey Royal, although the knobbly Pink Fir Apple is staging a challenge. These potatoes are at their best in the spring and early summer.

Floury potatoes are main crop potatoes and are divided into categories according to their harvest time. They are available all year round but different varieties are available at different times of the year.

The flavour and texture of each type of potato varies a great deal, so experiment with different ones to find the kind you like the best. Today supermarkets often recommend cooking procedures for each type, but I have personal favourites. These are the potatoes I like to use:

Boiling: Jersey Royal, Pink Fir Apple, Ratte, Charlotte

Baking: Cara, Desiree

Mashing: Estima, Maris Piper

Sautéing: King Edward, Maris Piper

Roasting: King Edward, Maris Piper

Chipping: Maris Piper, Pentland Squire

To boil new potatoes, scrape the skins off or leave the skins on. Bring enough water to cover the potatoes to the boil. Tip in the potatoes, reduce the heat to a simmer and cook until tender. Drain and allow to steam dry for 2 minutes. A few sprigs of mint placed over the hot potatoes will infuse them with their scent.

To boil floury potatoes, peel and cut them into 5 cm (2in) pieces. Place them in a large saucepan and cover with water. Salt liberally. Cover with a lid and bring to the boil then reduce the heat to a simmer. Cook until a table knife can be inserted easily. Drain in a colander and allow to steam dry for 2 minutes.

SPICY POTATO WEDGES

Pre-heat the oven to 200°C, 400°F, Gas 6. Peel the potatoes and cut lengthways into wedges.

In a large bowl, mix together the remaining ingredients and use to coat the potato wedges.

Cover a baking sheet with lightly oiled foil. Tip the potato wedges on to the foil-lined sheet in a single layer, then roast in the oven for 1 hour, or until well browned and tender when pierced with a knife. The potatoes can be kept warm in a low oven, uncovered, for up to 1 hour. Serve hot.

135 CALS PER PORTION • 4 G FAT PER PORTION • PREPARATION TIME: 10 MIN • COOKING TIME: 1 HR • CAN BE MADE 6 HR AHEAD • FREEZE-ABILITY: NOT ADVISABLE.

SERVES 6-8

900 g (2 lb) baking potatoes

30 g (1 oz) sachet of coconut cream
   or 2 fl oz (60 ml) coconut milk

¼ tsp garlic granules

½ tsp salt

1 tsp ground lemon grass

½ tsp ground cumin

½ tsp ground coriander

½ tsp ground turmeric

¼ tsp hot chilli powder to taste

1 tbsp sesame oil

These potatoes make a great side dish for meats and vegetables.

POMMES BOULANGERE

Pre-heat the oven to 170°C, 325°F, Gas 3. Melt 40 g (1½ oz) of butter in a small saucepan and stir in the onion. Place a piece of damp greaseproof paper on the onion and cover with a lid. Cook over a low heat for about 20 minutes, or until the onion has softened. Remove the paper and lid, stir in the garlic and cook for a further minute.

Peel the potatoes and slice very thinly. Grease a large ovenproof dish with butter and arrange the potatoes in layers in the dish, along with the onion and a little salt and pepper. Arrange the top layer of potatoes in overlapping slices.

Dot the potatoes with the remaining butter and pour over the stock. Press the potatoes down firmly – they should be completely submerged in the stock. Cook in the oven for about 1½ hours, or until the potatoes are tender and browned on top.

If made in advance, reheat at 170°C, 325°F, Gas 3 for 30 minutes.

139 CALS PER PORTION • 6 G FAT PER PORTION • PREPARATION TIME: 25 MIN • COOKING TIME: 1½ HR • CAN BE MADE A DAY AHEAD • FREEZE-ABILITY: 3 MONTHS.

SERVES 6 8

55 g (2 oz) butter

1 large onion, very thinly sliced

1 clove garlic, crushed

900 g (2 lb) floury potatoes

Butter for greasing

Salt and ground black pepper

425 ml (¾ pt) well-seasoned chicken
   or vegetable stock

Cut individual portions with a scone-cutter for a smart restaurant-style presentation.

Add some crunch to your new potatoes by sautéing them just before serving.

SAUTÉED NEW POTATOES

SERVES 6-8

Cook the potatoes in boiling salted water for 20 minutes until soft when pierced with a sharp knife. Drain, peel and cut in half lengthways.

900 g (2 lb) new potatoes, unscraped

4 tbsp olive oil

30 g (1 oz) butter

Salt and ground black pepper

Heat the oil in a large sauté pan. Add the butter, heat until starting to brown, then fry the potatoes for 1 minute on each side. Season. Keep warm in an oven pre-heated to 150°C, 300°F, Gas 2 for up to 30 minutes.

195 CALS PER PORTION • 9 G FAT PER PORTION • PREPARATION TIME: 5 MIN • COOKING TIME: 25 MIN • CAN BE MADE 30 MIN AHEAD • FREEZE-ABILITY: CANNOT BE FROZEN.

GARLIC AND OLIVE OIL

MASHED POTATOES

Peel the potatoes, cut into even-sized chunks about 6 x 4 cm (2½ x 1¼ in) and put immediately into a large saucepan with enough cold salted water to cover them. Add the garlic, bring to the boil, turn down the heat and simmer for about 10 minutes.

Meanwhile, wash the spring onions and slice the white and tender green parts at an angle into 0.5 cm (¼ in) pieces. Heat the oil and cook the spring onion slices over a low heat for about 3 minutes until softened, or until tender when pierced with a knife.

Drain the potatoes through a sieve and leave for 2 minutes to steam dry. Purée the potatoes and the garlic whilst still warm by pushing them through a sieve with a wooden spoon.

Add the milk to the spring onions in the oil, heat until warmed through then beat into the sieved potatoes and season to taste. Serve.

294 CALS PER PORTION • 8 G FAT PER PORTION • PREPARATION TIME: 10 MIN • COOKING TIME: 20 MIN• CAN BE MADE A DAY AHEAD • FREEZE-ABILITY: NOT ADVISABLE.

SERVES 6-8

900 g (2 lb) floury potatoes
Salt and ground black pepper
2 cloves garlic, peeled
1 bunch of spring onions
4 tbsp extra-virgin olive oil
6 tbsp milk

Never add cold milk to potatoes as they will become gluey. This dish can be made in advance and reheated in a microwave or in an oven pre-heated to 150°C, 300°F, Gas 3. Alternatively, cover the potatoes with a thin layer of milk and some foil and keep them hot for 1 hour at 100°C, 200°F, Gas 1.

TWO-POTATO GALETTE

SERVES 6

55 g (2 oz) butter
1 clove garlic, crushed
450 g (1 lb) Maris Piper potatoes
450 g (1 lb) red-fleshed sweet potatoes
Salt and ground black pepper

An easy-to-make potato cake. Cook it early in the day for reheating, or keep it warm in a low oven.

Pre-heat the oven to 200°C, 400°F, Gas 6. Grease a 20 cm (8 in) diameter cake tin or ovenproof dish with a little of the butter and line the base with baking parchment. Melt the remaining butter in a small pan and add the garlic.

Peel and cut the potatoes into 3 mm (⅛ in) slices. Layer alternating types in the dish, seasoning each layer with salt, pepper and the garlic butter.

Cover with buttered foil and bake for 1¼ hours, or until tender when pierced with a knife. Invert the galette on to a plate and serve hot. Brown the top briefly under the grill if necessary.

190 CALS PER PORTION • 8 G FAT PER PORTION • PREPARATION TIME: 10 MIN • COOKING TIME: 75 MIN • CAN BE MADE 8 HR AHEAD • FREEZE-ABILITY: NOT ADVISABLE.

CANDIED SWEET POTATOES

SERVES 8

1 kg (2¼ lb) sweet potatoes
1 tsp salt
55 g (2 oz) butter
150 ml (¼ pt) maple syrup
110 g (4 oz) golden marmalade
Salt and ground black pepper
2 tbsp demerara sugar
55 g (2 oz) pecans, coarsely chopped
1 tbsp chopped fresh parsley, to garnish

In the USA this is a popular way of preparing this native American vegetable.

Pre-heat the oven to 190°C, 375°F, Gas 5. Peel the potatoes, cut into 5 cm (2 in) chunks and place in a large saucepan of cold water. Add the salt, cover and bring to the boil. Simmer for about 12 minutes or until tender. Drain through a sieve and place in a bowl.

Melt the butter, then stir in the maple syrup and marmalade. Pour over the potatoes, stirring to coat.

Transfer to an ovenproof dish. Season, then sprinkle over the sugar and pecans. Cook on the top shelf for 45 minutes until browned. Serve immediately, garnished with chopped parsley.

296 CALS PER PORTION • 11 G FAT PER PORTION • PREPARATION TIME: 20 MIN • COOKING TIME: 45 MIN • CAN BE MADE A DAY AHEAD • FREEZE-ABILITY: NOT ADVISABLE.

POMMES DAUPHINOISE

Melt the butter in a saucepan over a medium-low heat, then stir in the onion. Place a piece of damp greaseproof paper on top of the onion, then cover the pan. Cook for about 20 minutes, until the onion is very soft. Stir occasionally, taking care it doesn't burn.

Peel the potatoes and cut into 0.25 cm (¼ in) thick slices. Do not soak them in water, as the starch will help make the sauce creamy.

Remove the lid and paper from the onion and stir in the garlic. Cook for a further 2 minutes, then stir in the remaining ingredients and season.

Stir to coat the potatoes with the cream mixture. Cook until the potatoes are just soft (test by piercing with the point of a sharp knife). Check the seasoning and adjust if necessary.

Turn the potatoes into a large, shallow and buttered ovenproof dish. If you're preparing them ahead, they should be cooled and chilled at this point.

To cook the potatoes, pre-heat the oven to 180°C, 350°F, Gas 4. Bake in the middle of the oven for 45 minutes or until they are browned on top and very soft when pierced with a knife.

457 CALS PER PORTION • 32 G FAT PER PORTION • PREPARATION TIME: 35 MIN • COOKING TIME: 1 HR •
CAN BE MADE A DAY AHEAD • FREEZE-ABILITY: CANNOT BE FROZEN.

SERVES 8

30 g (1 oz) butter
225 g (8 oz) onion, finely sliced
1 kg (2¼ lb) floury potatoes,
   such as Maris Piper
2 cloves garlic, crushed
290 ml (½ pt) milk
290 ml (½ pt) single cream
400 g (14 fl oz) crème fraîche
Salt and ground black pepper

This classic French potato recipe is always a firm favourite.

Rosti, meaning crisp and golden, is a Swiss method of preparing potatoes. They can be prepared a day in advance and turned out, then reheated on a baking sheet for 30 minutes at 180°C, 350°F, Gas 4. Floury white potatoes can also be used in this recipe.

SWEET POTATO ROSTI

SERVES 6–8

1 kg (2¼ lb) red-fleshed sweet potatoes or floury white potatoes such as Maris Piper

85 g (3 oz) butter, melted

1 bunch of spring onions, chopped

Salt and ground black pepper

Pre-heat the oven to 200°C, 400°F, Gas 6. Peel the potatoes and cut into 7 cm (3 in) pieces.

Place in a large saucepan with 1 tsp of salt and cover with cold water. Bring to the boil, then simmer for 5 minutes. Drain, then stand until cool enough to handle.

Use some of the butter to grease eight Yorkshire pudding tins or a 30 cm (12 in) ovenproof sauté pan.

Grate the potatoes coarsely, stir in the remaining butter and the spring onions. Season. Press the potatoes into the tins or pan.

If using the pudding tins, place in the oven and bake for 45 minutes or until golden brown. If using the frying pan, cook over a medium heat until brown on the bottom, then place in the oven for 30 minutes or until golden on top. Turn out to serve.

254 CALS PER PORTION • 12 G FAT PER PORTION • PREPARATION TIME: 25 MIN • COOKING TIME: 45 MIN • CAN BE MADE A DAY AHEAD • FREEZE-ABILITY: 3 MONTHS.

CHAPTER TEN

PASTA AND GRAINS

TABBOULEH

SERVES 8

170 g (6 oz) bulghur wheat

1 cucumber, peeled, de-seeded and finely sliced

1 bunch of spring onions, finely diced

6 tbsp finely chopped fresh parsley

3 tbsp finely chopped fresh mint

Juice of 1 lemon

4 tbsp olive oil

$\frac{1}{2}$ tsp salt

Freshly ground black pepper

2 Little Gem lettuces

A classic Middle Eastern salad which can be used as an accompaniment for grilled meats and fish.

Place the bulgar wheat in a bowl then pour over boiling water and leave to stand for 30 minutes.

Drain the bulghur wheat and squeeze in a tea towel to remove excess moisture.

Transfer to a bowl and stir in all the remaining ingredients except the lettuce.

Separate the lettuce leaves and use to line a serving dish. Pile the salad on to the lettuce leaves to serve.

151 CALS PER PORTION • 7 G FAT PER PORTION • PREPARATION TIME: 35 MIN • COOKING TIME: NONE • CAN BE MADE A DAY AHEAD • FREEZE-ABILITY: NOT ADVISABLE.

THAI NOODLES

Place the mushrooms in a bowl and cover with boiling water. Leave for 20 minutes.

Heat a little of the oil in a small frying pan and use the egg mixture to make 4 thin omelettes. Cut the omelettes into thin strips and set aside.

Cook the noodles, according to the packet instructions, drain well and toss with 1 tbsp of oil. Drain the mushrooms and slice thinly. Set both aside.

Mix the lime juice with the soy sauce, fish sauce and sugar.

Heat the remaining oil in a large wok or frying pan. Add the ginger, shallots, garlic and chillies and cook, stirring, over a medium heat for 2 minutes. Add the noodles and stir to coat with the oil. Stir in the soy sauce mixture. Add the mushrooms, egg strips, beansprouts, and half of the coriander, peanuts and spring onions. Toss and continue to cook for 5 minutes until warmed through.

Turn into warmed serving bowls and garnish with the remaining coriander, peanuts and onions.

565 CALS PER PORTION • 32 G FAT PER PORTION • PREPARATION TIME: 20 MIN • COOKING TIME: 10 MIN • CAN BE MADE A DAY AHEAD (IF SERVED AS A COLD SALAD) • FREEZE-ABILITY: NOT ADVISABLE.

SERVES 8

40 g (1½ oz) dried shiitake mushrooms
120 ml (4 fl oz) groundnut oil
2 medium eggs, beaten with
  1 tsp soy sauce
500 g (1 lb 2 oz) medium egg noodles
Juice of 2 limes
120 ml (4 fl oz) soy sauce
4 tbsp fish sauce
1 tbsp caster sugar
1 tbsp grated fresh ginger
4 shallots, finely chopped
4 cloves garlic, crushed
2 red chillies, de-seeded and finely diced
200 g (7 oz) beansprouts
1 tbsp chopped fresh coriander
200g (7 oz) peanuts, chopped
½ bunch of spring onions, sliced

These quick-to-cook noodles are a great way to satisfy hungry vegetarians.

CORIANDER CRACKED WHEAT SALAD

SERVES 8

170 g (6 oz) cracked wheat or
bulghur wheat
½ tsp salt
4 medium tomatoes, peeled, de-seeded
and cut into 5 mm (¼ in) dice
½ cucumber, de-seeded and cut
into 5 mm (¼ in) dice
1 to 2 tbsp lemon juice
2 tbsp finely chopped fresh coriander
2 tbsp finely chopped fresh parsley
1 bunch of spring onions, chopped
4 tbsp olive oil
Salt and ground black pepper
1 head of Cos lettuce, shredded

Place the cracked wheat or bulgar wheat in a saucepan with the salt and 570 ml (1 pt) water. Bring to the boil and simmer for 10 minutes (the wheat should still have some 'bite' to it). Drain in a sieve and allow to steam. Stand until cool.

Squeeze the wheat in a clean tea towel to remove any excess moisture and place in a bowl. Stir in all the remaining ingredients, except the lettuce, season and store in the fridge until needed.

To serve, line a large serving plate with the lettuce and top with the salad.

140 CALS PER PORTION • 6 G FAT PER PORTION • PREPARATION TIME: 20 MIN • COOKING TIME: 15 MIN • CAN BE MADE A DAY AHEAD • FREEZE-ABILITY: CANNOT BE FROZEN.

Make this refreshing salad as an accompaniment to Thai Green Curry Chicken Salad (see recipe on page 55).

This pale golden, saffron-scented pilaf originated in Turkey.

SAFFRON RICE AND PASTA PILAF

Cover the rice with cold water and set aside.

Heat the oil and butter in a saucepan over a low heat, stir in the onions, cover with a piece of damp greaseproof paper on top of the onions and then cover with a lid. Cook for 5 minutes until the onions are soft, remove the paper and lid, and add the vermicelli. Continue to cook over a medium heat until the onions and pasta turn golden.

Drain the rice in a sieve, rinse under the cold tap and drain well. Add to the onion mixture and stir to coat the rice with oil. Cook for 1 minute or until the grains of rice turn opaque.

Place the stock in a jug and add the saffron. Taste and adjust the seasoning – it should be well seasoned. Add to the rice, bring to the boil and lower the heat so the liquid just simmers. Cover and cook for about 15 minutes until the surface of the rice looks dry and holes appear.

Spread a clean, unfolded tea towel over the saucepan and replace the lid on top, folding the cloth back on top of the lid so it cannot catch alight. Continue to cook for a further 5 minutes over a low heat. Fluff with a fork, spread in a serving dish and sprinkle with parsley to serve.

SERVES 6

170 g (6 oz) long-grain rice

1 tbsp oil

15 g (½ oz) butter

110 g (4 oz) onions, chopped

55 g (2 oz) vermicelli, broken into
   2 cm (¾ in) lengths

¼ tsp saffron powder or pinch of
   saffron strands

570 ml (1 pt) chicken or vegetable stock

Salt and ground black pepper

2 tbsp chopped fresh parsley

182 CALS PER PORTION • 4 G FAT PER PORTION • PREPARATION TIME: 10 MIN • COOKING TIME: 35 MIN • CAN BE MADE A DAY AHEAD • FREEZE-ABILITY: 1 MONTH.

PASTA AND GRAINS   117

THAI RICE SALAD

SERVES 6

340 g (12 oz) jasmine rice

1 tbsp green cardamom pods

1 tsp whole cloves

1 cinnamon stick, broken

2 tsp salt

DRESSING

2 tbsp lemon juice

5 tbsp vegetable oil

4 spring onions, chopped

Wash the rice in several changes of water until all the starch has disappeared and the water is clear.

Place the rice, cardamom, cloves, cinnamon and salt in a saucepan with 1.5 ltr (2½ pt) water. Bring to the boil and cook for 8 minutes. Drain well. The spices can be removed at this point if desired.

Stir together all the dressing ingredients and pour over the rice. Chill until required.

292 CALS PER PORTION • 10 G FAT PER PORTION • PREPARATION TIME: 10 MIN • COOKING TIME: 10 MIN • CAN BE MADE A DAY AHEAD • FREEZE-ABILITY: CANNOT BE FROZEN.

For an authentic Thai touch, serve the rice salad in hollowed pineapple shells.

SESAME RICE

SERVES 6

340 g (12 oz) long-grain rice

55 g (2 oz) sesame seeds

2 tbsp sesame or vegetable oil

1 tbsp finely chopped, fresh coriander

Salt and ground black pepper

4 spring onions, finely chopped

Bring a large saucepan of salted water to the boil. Stir in the rice, bring back to the boil, then simmer for 10 minutes or until just tender.

Meanwhile, fry the sesame seeds in a frying pan with 1 tbsp of oil until lightly browned.

Rinse the rice with plenty of hot water to remove any excess starch and drain well, turning over occasionally with a fork to allow trapped steam to escape. Stir in the sesame seeds and coriander. Season to taste.

Place the remaining oil in a frying pan over a medium heat. Fry the spring onions for 2 minutes, until tender. Place the rice on serving plates, and garnish with the spring onions.

294 CALS PER PORTION • 10 G FAT PER PORTION • PREPARATION TIME: 5 MIN • COOKING TIME: 10 MIN • CAN BE MADE A DAY AHEAD • FREEZE-ABILITY: 1 MONTH.

This is a deliciously nutty-flavoured rice. Serve as a accompaniment to the Soy Braised Guinea Fowl with Shiitake Mushrooms (see recipe on page 59).

GREEN VEGETABLE PASTA SALAD

Purée the vinegar, garlic and basil in a liquidiser, then slowly add the oil whilst the motor is running. Whiz in the Parmesan. Season.

Cut the asparagus into 2 cm (¾ in) pieces and steam until for about 3 minutes until tender. Place in a colander and hold under cold running water for 10 seconds to cool. Drain well and set aside.

Cut the broccoli into bite-sized pieces and cook in boiling salted water for about 4 minutes until just tender. Place in a colander and hold under cold running water for 10 seconds to cool. Drain well and set aside.

Cook the pasta in plenty of boiling salted water until it is tender but still has some 'bite'. Drain well, transfer to a serving dish and stir the dressing into the hot pasta. Toss in the vegetables, pepper and olives. Chill in the fridge until required. To serve, adjust the seasoning and stir in the pine nuts.

315 CALS PER PORTION • 17 G FAT PER PORTION • PREPARATION TIME: 25 MIN • COOKING TIME: 20 MIN • CAN BE MADE A DAY AHEAD • FREEZE-ABILITY: NOT ADVISABLE.

SERVES 8

450 g (1 lb) fresh asparagus

450 g (1 lb) broccoli

450 g (1 lb) fusilli pasta

1 yellow pepper, de-seeded and chopped

140 g (5 oz) pitted black olives, shredded

100 g (3½ oz) pine nuts, toasted

DRESSING

60 ml (2 fl oz) balsamic vinegar

1 large clove garlic

30 g (1 oz) fresh basil leaves

150 ml (¼ pt) olive oil

30 g (1 oz) freshly grated Parmesan cheese

Salt and ground black pepper

This herby pasta salad is a firm favourite with vegetarians and carnivores alike.

LEMON COUSCOUS

SERVES 6

255 g (9 oz) couscous

1 tsp salt

225 g (8 oz) orange-fleshed sweet potato

Salt and ground black pepper

225 g (8 oz) courgettes, cut into 5 mm (¼ in) cubes

150 ml (¼ pt) olive oil

425 g (15 oz) canned chickpeas, drained and rinsed

Grated zest and juice of 1 lemon

1 tbsp chopped fresh coriander

Place the couscous and salt in a bowl and pour over enough cold water to cover the couscous by 1 cm (½ in). Leave to stand for 30 minutes, stirring occasionally with a fork.

Meanwhile, peel the potato and cut into 1 cm (½ in) chunks. Place in a saucepan with a pinch of salt and cover with cold water. Bring to the boil and simmer for 10 minutes, or until tender when pierced with a knife. Drain and leave to cool.

Sauté the courgettes in 2 tbsp of olive oil for about 1 minute until lightly browned. Set aside.

Drain the couscous, then stir in the potato, courgettes, chickpeas, lemon zest and juice and remaining olive oil. Season and chill until required.

Just before serving, place the couscous in a colander over a saucepan of simmering water. Cover and steam for 10 minutes, stirring occasionally with a fork. Just before serving, stir in the coriander and turn into a bowl.

387 CALS PER PORTION • 24 G FAT PER PORTION • PREPARATION TIME: 40 MIN • COOKING TIME: 10 MIN TO REHEAT • CAN BE MADE A DAY AHEAD • FREEZE-ABILITY: CANNOT BE FROZEN.

Couscous, a staple of north African cooking, is granular semolina which has been pre-cooked. Soaking the couscous in cold instead of hot water gives a lighter texture.

CHAPTER ELEVEN

PUDDINGS

CITRUS JELLY TERRINE

SERVES 8

285 g (10 oz) granulated sugar

2 pink grapefruit

2 white grapefruit

4 large oranges

2 tbsp gelatine

2 oranges, segmented, and 8 mint sprigs, to decorate

This is an impressive fat-free dessert.

Place the sugar in a saucepan, cover with 290 ml (½ pt) warm water and dissolve over a low heat. Pare the zest from 1 grapefruit and 1 orange and add to the pan while the sugar is dissolving. When it has dissolved, bring the syrup to the boil and bubble for 5 minutes. Allow to stand for 20 minutes to infuse.

Discard the pith and peel from all the fruit, cut into segments and set aside. Add any juice to the sugar syrup, then strain the syrup into a measuring jug. Make the quaintity up to 570 ml (1 pt) with cold water.

Place 60 ml (2 fl oz) water in a small saucepan. Sprinkle the gelatine on to the water, leave to stand for 5 minutes, then dissolve the gelatin over a low heat and add to the syrup. Leave to stand until the liquid starts to set.

Pour a thin layer of the jelly into a 1.2 ltr (2 pt) loaf tin. Stand the tin in an ice bath to help it set. Place a layer of fruit over the jelly while it is still tacky. Pour a little more jelly over the fruit and continue layering the fruit and jelly until all the fruit has been used. Pour a thin layer of jelly over the fruit to finish.

Chill the terrine for at least 4 hours before serving. Store in the fridge until needed.

To serve, dip the tin into hand-hot water for 10 seconds, then turn on to a serving dish. Serve the jelly cut into slices, decorated with orange segments and mint sprigs.

211 CALS PER PORTION • 0 G FAT PER PORTION • PREPARATION TIME: 40 MIN. PLUS 4 HR CHILLING TIME • CAN BE MADE 3 DAYS AHEAD • FREEZE-ABILITY: NOT ADVISABLE.

TROPICAL CITRUS SALAD

If the fruit is tart, sprinkle with the sugar. Layer the oranges, pineapple and coconut in a large glass serving dish, finishing with the coconut. Sprinkle with the wine or orange juice.

Cover with clingfilm and chill for 6 hours or overnight. Serve with Gingerbread Cookies (see recipe below).

238 CALS PER PORTION • 12 G FAT PER PORTION • PREPARATION TIME: 25 MIN. PLUS 6 HR CHILLING TIME • CAN BE MADE A DAY AHEAD • FREEZE-ABILITY: NOT ADVISABLE.

SERVES 8

6 large navel oranges, peeled and sliced

1 large pineapple, peeled,
   cored and shredded

55 g (2 oz) caster sugar (optional)

255 g (9 oz) coconut shreds

90 ml (3 fl oz) Essensia wine
   or orange juice

Essensia is an amazing orange-blossom-scented wine that's magical when chilled.

GINGERBREAD COOKIES

Beat the butter, sugar and molasses in a bowl until fluffy. Gradually add the egg, beating well between each addition.

Sift together all the remaining ingredients, except the icing sugar, into a bowl. Stir into the butter mixture.

Press the dough into a flat layer between two sheets of greaseproof paper. Chill for about 1 hour until firm.

Pre-heat the oven to 190°C, 375°F, Gas 5. On a lightly floured surface, roll out the dough to 5mm (¼ in) thick for slightly soft cookies, thinner for very crisp cookies. Cut out cookie shapes and place on a lightly greased baking sheet, leaving 4 cm (1½ in) between each cookie. Chill until firm. If you want to hang them on a Christmas tree make a hole in the cookies before baking.

Bake in the middle of the oven for 8 to 10 minutes until the edges of the cookies are lightly browned. Cool for 1 minute, then transfer to a wire rack to cool completely. Dust with icing sugar before serving. Store in a airtight container.

76 CALS PER PORTION • 4 G FAT PER PORTION • PREPARATION TIME: 20 MIN, PLUS 1 HR CHILLING TIME • COOKING TIME: 10 MIN • CAN BE MADE 1 WEEK AHEAD • FREEZE-ABILITY: 1 MONTH.

MAKES ABOUT 48

225 g (8 oz) butter, softened

170 g (6 oz) light muscovado sugar

1 tbsp molasses

1 medium egg, beaten

340 g (12 oz) plain flour

1 tsp bicarbonate of soda

2 tsp ground cinnamon

1 tsp ground ginger

½ tsp salt

½ tsp ground cloves

Icing sugar, to dust

Shape the cookies as you wish. They can also be tied with a ribbon and used to decorate a Christmas tree.

AMARETTO AND APRICOT ZABAGLIONE

To make the apricot purée, place the apricots in a pan with the sugar, lemon zest and 290 ml (½ pt) water. Simmer over a medium-low heat for 15 minutes. Leave to cool.

Discard the lemon zest, then purée the apricots and liquid in a food processor or liquidiser. Adjust the flavour to taste with extra sugar or lemon juice. Set aside.

For the zabaglione, place 3 tbsp cold water in a small pan and sprinkle the gelatine on to the water. Leave to dissolve.

Place the egg yolks and sugar in a large bowl, then set over a pan of simmering water and whisk for 10 minutes until thick and mousse-like. Gradually whisk in the Amaretto, remove from the heat and continue to whisk for about 5 minutes until the mixture cools to room temperature.

Place the pan containing dissolved gelatine over a low heat until clear, then stir into the zabaglione mixture. Stir occasionally until thickened.

Meanwhile, whip the cream in a bowl until softly peaking, then fold into the zabaglione mixture.

Spoon the apricot purée and zabaglione alternately into tall glasses and run a knife through the mixture to create a marbled effect. Chill for at least 4 hours or overnight. Serve with Pine Nut Macaroons (see recipe below).

SERVES 8

1 tsp gelatine
5 egg yolks
85 g (3 oz) caster sugar
60 ml (2 fl oz) Amaretto liqueur
240 ml (8 fl oz) whipping cream
APRICOT PURÉE
170 g (6 oz) dried apricots
30 g (1 oz) caster sugar
1 strip of lemon zest

The addition of gelatine means this dessert can be made in advance. However, raw eggs shouldn't be eaten by young children, the elderly or pregnant women.

257 CALS PER PORTION • 15 G FAT PER PORTION • PREPARATION TIME: 30 MIN • COOKING TIME: 30 MIN •
CAN BE MADE A DAY AHEAD • FREEZE-ABILITY: NOT ADVISABLE.

PINE NUT MACAROONS

Pre-heat the oven to 180°C, 350°F, Gas 4. Line two baking sheets with rice paper.

Mix together the almonds, sugar, vanilla essence and flour. Stir in the egg whites, whisk for 5 minutes, then leave to stand for 5 minutes. Whisk again for 5 minutes.

Spoon teaspoonfuls of the mixture on to the rice paper, then gently press the nuts on to the top of each pile. Bake in the centre of the oven for 20 minutes until golden, then transfer to a wire rack to cool.

Tear off and discard excess paper from around the edges of each biscuit and store in an airtight container until required.

MAKES ABOUT 24

110 g (4 oz) ground almonds
170 g (6 oz) caster sugar
2 drops of vanilla essence
1 tsp plain flour
2 egg whites
100 g (3½ oz) pine nuts

Deliciously nutty, these biscuits are a delight.

88 CALS PER PORTION • 5 G FAT PER PORTION • PREPARATION TIME: 20 MIN • COOKING TIME: 20 MIN •
CAN BE MADE 1 WEEK AHEAD • FREEZE-ABILITY: NOT ADVISABLE.

EXOTIC FRUIT PLATTER

SERVES 6

Selection of fruit, such as pineapple, mango, papaya, kiwi, strawberries

SYRUP

140 g (5 oz) golden caster sugar

Pared zest and juice of 1 lime

1 star anise pod

1 cinnamon stick, broken into 3

7 whole cloves

5 cardamom pods

1 tsp coriander seeds

1 vanilla pod

2 tbsp Malibu liqueur

The syrup can be made up to a week in advance. Prepare the fruit platter on the day of serving – it makes a great dish for entertaining.

To make the syrup, place all the ingredients, except the liqueur, in a saucepan with 290 ml (½ pt) water. Heat over a low heat until the sugar has dissolved. Turn up the heat and boil the syrup for 5 minutes.

Allow the syrup to cool then sieve to remove the spices. Add the liqueur.

Peel and slice the fruits and arrange on a serving dish. Pour over the syrup and chill for at least 1 hour before serving.

Serve with Lime and Coconut Tuiles (see recipe opposite).

162 CALS PER PORTION • 0.4 G FAT PER PORTION • PREPARATION TIME: 25 MIN • COOKING TIME: 10 MIN • SYRUP CAN BE MADE 1 WEEK AHEAD • FREEZE-ABILITY: CANNOT BE FROZEN.

LIME AND COCONUT TUILES

Melt the butter and set it aside to cool.

Pre-heat the oven to 190°C, 375°F, Gas 5. Line a baking sheet with silicon paper.

In a large bowl, whisk the egg white until stiff then whisk in the caster sugar. Fold in the other ingredients, including the cooled butter.

Spread the mixture on to the paper-lined baking sheet in very thin 10 cm (3 in) rounds.

Bake in the oven for 5 to 6 minutes or until golden brown around the edges and opaque in the centre.

Lightly oil the handle of a wooden spoon and curl the warm tuiles around it. When set, ease them from the handle on to a wire rack to cool.

CALS PER PORTION : 61 • 4 G FAT PER PORTION • PREPARATION TIME: 10 MIN • COOKING TIME: 15 MIN • CAN BE MADE 1 WEEK AHEAD • FREEZE-ABILITY: CAN BE FROZEN IN A PLASTIC CONTAINER FOR UP TO 1 MONTH.

MAKES ABOUT 12

30 g (1 oz) butter
1 egg white
55 g (2 oz) caster sugar
30 g (1 oz) plain flour
Grated zest of 1 lime
2 tbsp desiccated coconut

Once you've got the hang of shaping these wafer-thin biscuits, try experimenting with different shapes.

INDIVIDUAL BERRY SOUFFLES

Butter eight 290 ml (½ pt) soufflé dishes and dust each with caster sugar. Purée the drained fruit in a liquidiser, then pass through a sieve.

Pre-heat the oven, and a baking sheet, to 200°C, 400°F, Gas 6.

Mix half the caster sugar with the flour in a saucepan, then pour in a little of the milk to form a smooth paste. Add the remaining milk and stir over a medium heat until the mixture comes to the boil. Boil for 1 minute.

Beat the egg yolks in a large bowl, then stir in the milk mixture, a little at a time. Next, stir in the fruit purée.

Whisk the egg whites until very stiff in a clean, dry bowl, then whisk in the remaining caster sugar, 1 tsp at a time. Fold a large spoonful of whites into the purée to loosen it, then carefully fold in the rest.

Turn the mixture into the soufflé dishes. Run the edge of a table knife around the edge of each dish, cutting into the mixture by 5 mm (¼ in).

Place on the pre-heated baking sheet and bake for 12 to 14 minutes in the top of the oven, until risen but wobbly when shaken gently. Dust with icing sugar, pour Grand Marnier into the centre, if desired, and serve immediately.

COOK'S TIP The soufflés can be frozen in their dishes for up to a week – cover with clingfilm first. To serve, bake as above for 25 to 30 minutes.

192 CALS PER PORTION • 6 G FAT PER PORTION • PREPARATION TIME: 15 MIN • COOKING TIME: 15 MIN • PUREE AND BASE CAN BE MADE A DAY AHEAD • FREEZE-ABILITY: 1 WEEK.

SERVES 8

Butter and caster sugar for the
soufflé dishes

500 g (1 lb 2 oz) frozen mixed red fruit,
defrosted and drained

110 g (4 oz) caster sugar

30 g (1 oz) plain flour

190 ml (6 fl oz) milk

4 medium egg yolks

6 medium egg whites

Icing sugar, to dust

8 tbsp Grand Marnier (optional)

These soufflés make an elegant dessert at any time of the year.

MULLED WINE PEARS

SERVES 8

570 ml (1 pt) red wine
225 g (8 oz) granulated sugar
Pared zest of 1 orange and 1 lemon
1 tsp whole cloves
1 cinnamon stick
2.5 cm (1 in) piece of fresh ginger,
peeled and thinly sliced
8 firm pears
Juice of 1 lemon

A neat and clean way
to remove the core from
the bottom of the pear is
with a melon baller.

Place the wine, sugar, zests and spices in a large saucepan with 290 ml (½ pt) water and heat gently until the sugar has dissolved. Bring to the boil and simmer for 5 minutes, then let the mixture stand for 10 minutes.

Peel the pears, without removing the stalks, and remove the cores through the base. Place the pears as you work in a bowl of water, adding the lemon juice to prevent discolouration.

Stand the pears upright in the saucepan containing the wine mixture and cover with greaseproof paper. The liquid should cover the pears completely – if it doesn't, the pears will have to be turned during cooking.

Bring the liquid to the boil, then simmer for 1 hour or until the pears are tender when pierced with a skewer. The cooking time depends on the ripeness of the pears.

Remove the pears from the pan and place them in a serving dish.

Reduce the cooking liquid by boiling it rapidly until it turns syrupy. Be careful not to let it burn. Pass the liquid through a sieve and pour over the pears. Leave to cool, then chill in the fridge.

Serve with Gingerbread Cookies (see recipe on page 123).

210 CALS PER PORTION • 0 G FAT PER PORTION • PREPARATION TIME: 15 MIN • COOKING TIME: 1 HR •
CAN BE MADE 3 DAYS AHEAD • FREEZE-ABILITY: CANNOT BE FROZEN.

CHOCOLATE PANNA COTTA

Lightly oil six 150 ml (¼ pt) dariole moulds.

Place 4 tbsp of milk in a saucepan and sprinkle over the powdered gelatine. Leave to stand for 5 minutes.

Combine the remaining milk with half the double cream and the chopped plain chocolate, and melt over a low heat, stirring frequently.

Dissolve the gelatine over a low heat until liquid. Do not let the milk boil.

Pour the gelatine and milk mixture immediately into the chocolate mixture, then stir in the Amaretto. Allow to cool, stirring occasionally until the mixture starts to set.

Whip the remaining double cream until soft peaks form. Fold into the chocolate mixture, then pour into the prepared dariole moulds. Tap the moulds to remove any air bubbles. Chill in the fridge for at least 4 hours.

To turn out, carefully dip the moulds into very hot water for about 10 seconds, then unmould them on to individual serving plates. Sprinkle crushed Amaretti biscuits over the top of each and serve with fresh raspberries.

412 CALS PER PORTION • 33 G FAT PER PORTION • PREPARATION TIME: 30 MIN • CHILLING TIME: 4 HR •
CAN BE MADE 2 DAYS AHEAD • FREEZE-ABILITY: 1 WEEK.

SERVES 6

240 ml (8 fl oz) milk
2 tsp gelatine
290 ml (½ pt) double cream
170 g (6 oz) plain chocolate, chopped
4 tbsp Amaretto liqueur
6 Amaretti biscuits, roughly crushed,
   to decorate
Fresh raspberries, to serve

Panna cotta is an easy-to-make classic Italian dessert. This chocolate version is particularly delicious.

This cheesecake is
very light and refreshing.

WHITE CHOCOLATE AND

MINT CHEESECAKE

SERVES 10

55 g (2 oz) butter, softened

15 g (½ oz) caster sugar

40 g (1½ oz) plain flour

15 g (½ oz) cocoa powder

30 g (1 oz) ground rice

100 g (3½ oz) minted milk chocolate

170 g (6 oz) good-quality white chocolate

450 g (1 lb) good-quality cream cheese

2 medium eggs, separated

150 ml (¼ pt) double cream

½ tsp peppermint extract

1 tbsp caster sugar

Cocoa powder and fresh mint sprigs,

to decorate

Pre-heat the oven to 180°C, 350°F, Gas 4. Beat together the butter and sugar in a bowl until light. Sift in the flour, cocoa and ground rice and mix together. Press the mixture into the base of a 20 cm (8 in) diameter loose-based tin and bake for 10 minutes. Leave to cool. Reduce the oven temperature to 130°C, 250°F, Gas 1.

Chop half the minted chocolate into small pieces. Melt the remainder and use to brush over the biscuit base.

Melt the white chocolate in a bowl over a pan of simmering water.

Meanwhile, beat the cream cheese in a bowl until it becomes thin. Beat in the egg yolks, cream and peppermint extract. Stir in the melted white chocolate, then the chopped mint chocolate.

Whisk the egg whites until stiff, whisk in the caster sugar, then fold the whites into the cheese mixture. Spread the filling over the biscuit base and bake in the middle of the oven for 50 minutes. Turn off the heat (the centre will still be very wobbly) and leave in the oven with the door ajar for 1 hour. Remove, cool and chill overnight in the fridge.

To serve, decorate the cheesecake with cocoa powder and mint sprigs.

502 CALS PER PORTION • 43 G FAT PER PORTION • PREPARATION TIME: 30 MIN • COOKING TIME: 1 HR PLUS
1 HR STANDING • CAN BE MADE 2 DAYS AHEAD • FREEZE-ABILITY:1 MONTH

MARBLED CHOCOLATE CHEESECAKE

SERVES 8

170 g (6 oz) double chocolate digestive
biscuits, crushed

55g (2 oz) butter, melted

675 g (1½ lb) full-fat cream cheese

175 g (6oz) caster sugar

3 medium eggs, beaten

4 tbsp double cream

1 tsp vanilla essence

3 tbsp cocoa powder

½ tsp instant coffee powder

This rich and
chocolatey cheesecake
is impressively marbled.

Pre-heat the oven to 140°C, 275°F, Gas 1. Combine the crushed biscuits with the butter in a bowl and press the mixture into the base of a 20 cm (8 in) diameter loose-based deep cake tin. Refrigerate until required.

Beat the cream cheese and sugar together until very soft, then beat in the eggs a little at a time. Stir in the cream and vanilla essence and divide between two bowls.

Mix the cocoa powder and coffee powder to a paste with 4 tbsp warm water and beat into the cream cheese mixture. Pour alternating cupfuls of the two mixtures slowly into the centre of the biscuit base.

When both mixtures are in the tin, pull a skewer from the centre through the filling to form a swirled pattern. Bake for 50 minutes, then turn off the oven and leave the cheesecake in it for a further hour.

Remove, cool and chill overnight in the fridge before serving.

716 CALS PER PORTION • 60 G FAT PER PORTION • PREPARATION TIME: 25 MIN • COOKING TIME: 50 MIN
PLUS 1 HR STANDING AND OVERNIGHT CHILLING • CAN BE MADE 3 DAYS AHEAD • FREEZE-ABILITY: 3 MONTHS.

PREVIOUS PAGE • MARBLED CHOCOLATE
CHEESECAKE

PANETTONE CHOCOLATE CHIP

BREAD PUDDING

Pre-heat the oven to 150°C, 300°F, Gas 2 and place a roasting tin half-filled with water (a bain-marie) in the oven. Butter a 1.5 ltr (2½ pt) shallow ovenproof dish, and scatter half the panettone over the base. Sprinkle with half the chocolate drops then add the remaining panettone.

Stir together the milk, both the creams, half the sugar, 3 whole eggs and 2 yolks. Stir in the Amaretto and vanilla essence, and sieve into a bowl. Whisk the 2 egg whites until just stiff, then fold them into the cream mixture and pour the mixture over the panettone. Top with the remaining chocolate drops and leave to stand for 30 minutes.

Sprinkle with the remaining sugar. Stand the dish in the bain-marie, and bake in the oven for 40 minutes until just set. Dust the pudding with cocoa and serve warm.

242 CALS PER PORTION • 16 G FAT PER PORTION • PREPARATION TIME: 20 MIN • COOKING TIME: 40 MIN • CAN BE MADE A DAY AHEAD • FREEZE-ABILITY: NOT ADVISABLE.

SERVES 6

Butter for greasing

225 g (8 oz) slightly stale panettone cake cut into 2.5 cm (1 in) chunks

55 g (2 oz) plain chocolate drops

290 ml (½ pt) milk

290 ml (½ pt) single cream

150 ml (¼ pt) double cream

55 g (2 oz) sugar

5 medium eggs

2 tbsp Amaretto liqueur

1 tsp vanilla essence

Sifted cocoa powder, for dusting

Panettone, the Italian yeast-raised cake found in most supermarkets, keeps this bread pudding extra light.

PISTACHIO PAVLOVAS WITH

RHUBARB AND RASPBERRIES

SERVES 6

3 egg whites

170 g (6 oz) caster sugar

1 tsp raspberry vinegar

1 tsp cornflour

100 g (3½ oz) shelled pistachio nuts, finely chopped

285 ml (10 fl oz) double cream

SAUCE

3 stalks young rhubarb

255 g (9 oz) frozen raspberries, defrosted

4 tbsp icing sugar

Using raspberry vinegar in a pavlova gives the meringue a lovely scent, but if you don't have any to hand, white wine vinegar can be used instead.

Pre-heat the oven to 130°C, 250°F, Gas 1, and line a baking tray with silicon paper on the reverse side of which you have marked six 7.5 cm (3 in) diameter circles.

Whisk the egg whites in a bowl until they are stiff, then start adding the caster sugar, 1 tbsp at a time, whisking well between each addition. When you have beaten in half the caster sugar in this way, fold in the rest in one batch with the vinegar, cornflour and all but 2 tbsp of the pistachio nuts.

Spread half the mixture over the six circles and mound the rest around the edges of the circles to form a cup shape. Sprinkle with the remaining nuts and bake for 1 hour. Leave to stand until cool.

To make the sauce, pre-heat the oven to 190°C, 375°F, Gas 5. Cut the rhubarb diagonally into small chunks and bake on a baking tray for 20 minutes or until tender. Leave to cool, then stir the rhubarb into the raspberries and sweeten to taste with the icing sugar.

To serve, whip the cream to soft peaks in a bowl, pile it into the pavlova cases and spoon the sauce over.

492 CALS PER PORTION • 32 G FAT PER PORTION • PREPARATION TIME: 20 MIN • COOKING TIME: 1½ HR • CAN BE MADE 1 WEEK AHEAD • FREEZE-ABILITY: 1 MONTH.

STRAWBERRY TIRAMISU

SERVES 6

340 g (12 oz) mascarpone cheese
2 tbsp single cream
85 g (3 oz) caster sugar
1 tsp vanilla essence
2 medium eggs, separated
85 ml (3 fl oz) white rum
85 ml (3 fl oz) milk
255 g (9 oz) sponge finger biscuits
450 g (1 lb) strawberries, washed and hulled
150 ml ($^{1}/_{4}$ pt) double cream
4 amaretti biscuits, roughly crushed, to decorate

This combination of strawberries, mascarpone and rum makes a delightful summer dessert.

Beat the mascarpone, single cream, sugar, vanilla essence and egg yolks together until light.

Whisk the egg whites until soft peaks form then fold them into the mascarpone mixture.

Mix the rum and milk in a saucer. One biscuit at a time, dip one-third of the sponge finger biscuits into the rum and milk and then use to line the base of a shallow serving dish. Cover the biscuit layer with half the mascarpone.

Reserve half the strawberries for decoration and slice the remainder. Place the sliced berries on top of the mascarpone.

Dip another third of the biscuits into the rum and milk and then layer them over the strawberries. Top with the remaining mascarpone.

Dip the remaining biscuits into the rum and milk and layer over them the mascarpone.

Whip the double cream until soft peaks form. Spread the cream over the biscuits.

Decorate the tiramisu with the halved strawberries and the crushed amaretti biscuits. Refrigerate for 2 weeks or overnight. Serve chilled.

350 CALS PER PORTION • 37 G FAT PER PORTION • PREPARATION TIME: 20 MIN • CAN BE MADE A DAY AHEAD • FREEZE-ABILITY: 1 MONTH.

STEAMED CRANBERRY PUDDINGS

WITH DARK CHOCOLATE CUSTARD

Line the bottom of six 150 ml (¼ pt) timbale moulds with discs of greaseproof paper and butter the moulds well.

Cream together the butter and sugar in a bowl until light, then add the beaten eggs, a spoonful at a time, beating well between each addition. Sift the flour over the top of the mixture and gently fold it in, then fold in the milk, vanilla essence, cranberries and chocolate drops.

Spoon the mixture into the moulds to fill each two-thirds full then cover with a disc of buttered foil, making a pleat in each piece of foil. Steam the puddings for 35 minutes in enough water to come halfway up the sides of the moulds. They will be firm to the touch when cooked.

Meanwhile, make the custard: melt the chocolate in the milk over a low heat, stirring occasionally. Mix the egg yolks and caster sugar in a bowl, then slowly stir in the warm chocolate milk. Return the mixture to the pan and stir over a medium heat until the custard thickens, but do not let it boil. Strain the custard into a serving bowl or jug.

Turn the cooked puddings out of the moulds, remove the paper discs and serve warm or at room temperature with the custard.

529 CALS PER PORTION • 31 G FAT PER PORTION • PREPARATION TIME: 30 MIN • COOKING TIME: 35 MIN • CAN BE MADE A DAY AHEAD • FREEZE-ABILITY: 1 MONTH.

SERVES 6

110 g (4 oz) butter, softened, plus
    butter for greasing
110 g (4 oz) caster sugar
2 medium eggs, beaten
110 g (4 oz) self-raising flour
3 tbsp milk
1 tsp vanilla essence
55 g (2 oz) frozen cranberries, defrosted
55 g (2 oz) white chocolate drops
CHOCOLATE CUSTARD
85 g (3 oz) plain chocolate,
    finely chopped
290 ml (½ pt) milk
3 egg yolks
1 tbsp caster sugar

Lovers of steamed puddings will adore these little cakes. If you don't have cranberries, raspberries make a perfect substitute.

OVERLEAF • STEAMED CRANBERRY PUDDING WITH DARK CHOCOLATE CUSTARD.

CHAPTER TWELVE

CAKES AND TARTS

MAPLE PECAN PIE

SERVES 8

110 g (4 oz) full-fat cream cheese
110 g (4 oz) butter, softened
170 g (6 oz) plain flour
Pinch of salt
FILLING
200 g (7 oz) pecan nuts
55 g (2 oz) butter
110g (4 oz) soft dark brown sugar
150 ml (¼ pt) pure maple syrup
150 ml (¼ pt) golden syrup
1 tsp vanilla essence
4 medium eggs, beaten
285 ml (10 fl oz) double cream, to serve

The maple syrup in the filling mellows the flavour without overwhelming the other tastes.

Mix together the cream cheese and butter, sift the flour and salt over them and stir until just combined. Between two sheets of clingfilm or greaseproof paper, roll out the pastry to a circle large enough to line a deep tart tin 23 cm (9 in) in diameter. Remove one sheet of clingfilm or greaseproof paper and use the other to help ease the pastry into the tin. Chill until firm.

To make the filling, put a baking sheet in the oven and pre-heat the oven to 200°C, 400°F, Gas 6. Set aside 110 g (4 oz) pecan nuts and coarsely chop the rest. Melt together the butter and sugar, then stir in the syrups, chopped nuts and vanilla essence. Leave to cool at room temperature then stir in the eggs.

Stand the lined tart tin on a baking sheet, pour in the filling and arrange the reserved pecans on top. Bake for 15 minutes then reduce the oven temperature to 180°C, 350°F, Gas 4 and bake for a further 30 to 40 minutes until the centre is just set. Serve warm or at room temperature with the double cream.

924 CALS PER PORTION • 62 G FAT PER PORTION • PREPARATION TIME: 15 MIN • COOKING TIME: 50 MIN • CAN BE MADE 2 DAYS AHEAD • FREEZE-ABILITY: 1 MONTH.

CHOCOLATE GINGER CAKE

SERVES 8

Pre-heat the oven to 180°C, 350°F, Gas 4. Line the base of a 20 cm (8 in) diameter springform tin with greaseproof paper and lightly oil the paper and the tin.

Put the chocolate in a bowl with the brandy or 2 tbsp water and the syrup and set over a pan of barely simmering water. When the chocolate has just melted, take it off the heat and stir in the butter.

Whisk the sugar and egg yolks in a large bowl until pale and thick, stir in the chocolate mixture and then fold in the ground almonds, flour, ginger and 2 tbsp warm water.

Whisk the egg whites until just stiff. Fold a spoonful into the chocolate mixture, then fold in the remainder. Turn the mixture into the tin and bake in the centre of the oven for 40 minutes (cover with greaseproof paper if browning too quickly). The cake will feel firm when done. Leave the cake in the tin on a wire rack to cool, then remove the tin and place the cake on the rack for glazing. If freezing, glaze and decorate the cake after defrosting.

To make the glaze, melt the chocolate in the brandy then stir in the butter as before. Quickly smooth the glaze over the cake. Arrange 'haystacks' of stem ginger on top and leave until the glaze has set.

610 CALS PER PORTION • 39 G FAT PER PORTION • PREPARATION TIME: 20 MIN • COOKING TIME: 40 MIN • CAN BE MADE 5 DAYS AHEAD • FREEZE-ABILITY: 1 MONTH.

Oil for greasing

200 g (7 oz) good-quality plain chocolate, chopped

2 tbsp brandy (optional)

1 tbsp syrup from preserved stem ginger

110 g (4 oz) butter, diced

140 g (5 oz) caster sugar

3 medium eggs, separated

100 g ($3\frac{1}{2}$ oz) ground almonds

55 g (2 oz) self-raising flour

2 pieces preserved stem ginger, chopped

GLAZE

140 g (5 oz) good-quality plain chocolate, chopped

1 tbsp brandy

40 g ($1\frac{1}{2}$ oz) butter, diced

1 piece preserved stem ginger, cut into fine strips

The festive flavours of chocolate and ginger combine to create a cake fit for any celebration.

TOASTED ALMOND ROULADE

WITH STRAWBERRIES AND CREAM

Pre-heat the oven to 190°C, 375°F, Gas 5. Line a 35 x 25 cm (14 x 10 in) roasting tin with baking parchment.

Toast the whole almonds on a baking sheet in the oven for 7 minutes until golden brown. Cool. Grind to a fine powder in a processor with 1 tbsp of caster sugar.

Reserve 1 tbsp of the remaining caster sugar for the egg whites and whisk the remainder with the egg yolks in a bowl until light and thick. Stir in the ground almond mixture.

Whisk the egg whites with a pinch of salt until just stiff, then beat in the reserved sugar. Stir a large spoonful of the whites into the almond mixture. Fold in the remaining egg whites carefully.

Turn the mixture into the prepared tin and sprinkle over half the flaked almonds. Cook in the oven for 12 to 15 minutes until golden brown and risen. Cool on a wire rack.

Dust a large piece of greaseproof paper with icing sugar. Turn out the roulade on to the paper.

Whip the cream until it just holds its shape and spread it over the roulade. Cover the cream with the strawberries, then roll the roulade up and place it on a serving dish. Decorate with the remaining flaked almonds, whole strawberries and mint sprigs.

383 CALS PER PORTION • 31 G FAT PER PORTION • PREPARATION TIME: 15 MIN • COOKING TIME: 15 MIN • CAN BE MADE A DAY AHEAD • FREEZE-ABILITY: CAKE (MINUS FILLING)1 MONTH.

SERVES 8

100 g (3½ oz) whole blanched almonds

100 g (3½ oz) caster sugar

4 medium eggs, separated

Pinch of salt

55 g (2 oz) flaked almonds

Icing sugar for dusting

290 ml (½ pt) double cream

225 g (8 oz) fresh strawberries,
   hulled and sliced

Whole strawberries and mint sprigs,
   to decorate

A roulade is a soufflé baked in a rectangular tin. It makes an incredibly light dessert.

STICKY FRUIT TART

SERVES 8

170 g (6 oz) plain flour
55 g (2 oz) ground rice
Pinch of salt
140 g (5 oz) butter
55 g (2 oz) golden caster sugar
1 egg, beaten
Single cream, to serve
TOPPING
40 g (1½ oz) butter
55 g (2 oz) golden caster sugar
255 g (9 oz) dried peaches
255 g (9 oz) dried figs
255 g (9 oz) dried apricots
100 g (3½ oz) dried cranberries

This delicious, sticky upside-down tart can be made entirely from store-cupboard ingredients.

Sift the flour, ground rice and salt into a large bowl. Rub in the butter until the mixture resembles breadcrumbs, then stir in the sugar and egg. Bring the pastry together with your hands, then roll between two sheets of clingfilm into a 25 cm (10 in) circle. Chill.

To make the topping, pre-heat the oven to 190°C, 375°F, Gas 5. Put the butter in a 25 cm (10 in) ceramic flan dish and place in the oven to melt. Remove the dish from the oven, then sprinkle with the sugar and arrange the fruit over the top.

Peel away and discard the clingfilm and place the pastry over the fruit, tucking down the edges. Bake in the centre of the oven for 30 to 40 minutes until the pastry is golden. Allow to stand for 2 minutes, then invert on to a serving dish. Serve warm with cream.

561 CALS PER PORTION • 21 G FAT PER PORTION • PREPARATION TIME: 20 MIN • COOKING TIME: 40 MIN • CAN BE MADE A DAY AHEAD • FREEZE-ABILITY: BEFORE BAKING 1 MONTH.

CHOCOLATE ORANGE MARBLED CAKE

Pre-heat the oven to 190°C, 375°F, Gas 5. Line the base of a 22 cm (9 in) round deep ring tin or 20 cm (8 in) round cake tin with greaseproof paper and grease lightly with a little of the butter.

Spread the hazelnuts on a baking sheet and bake for 8 minutes until lightly browned. Rub them in a tea towel to remove skins, leave to cool and grind in a coffee grinder or food processor.

Cream the butter, sugar and orange zest until pale and light. Beat in the eggs, 1 tbsp at a time. If the mixture starts to curdle beat in 1 tbsp of the flour.

Sift together the flour and baking powder. Fold this into the butter mixture along with the hazelnuts. Divide the mixture into two equal parts. Combine half the orange juice with the cocoa powder and fold into half the cake mixture. Fold the rest of the orange juice into the white cake mixture.

Place the two mixtures into the tin using alternate tablespoons. Tap the rim to level the mixtures, then use a skewer in a circular motion to marble through the surface of the two mixtures.

Bake in the centre of the oven for 45 minutes or until the cake is done – push a wooden skewer into the middle, it will come out clean if the cake is cooked.

498 CALS PER PORTION • 32 G FAT PER PORTION • PREPARATION TIME: 30 MIN • COOKING TIME: 45 MIN •
CAN BE MADE 5 DAYS AHEAD • FREEZE-ABILITY: 6 MONTHS.

SERVES 8

Oil for greasing
55 g (2 oz) hazelnuts
225 g (8 oz) butter, softened
225 g (8 oz) golden caster sugar
Grated zest and juice of 1 large orange
4 medium eggs, beaten
170 g (6 oz) self-raising flour
1 tsp baking powder
4 tbsp cocoa powder

A deliciously moist but not overly sweet cake.

MINCEMEAT TART

To make the pastry, sift the flour, salt and sugar into a large bowl or food processor. Rub the fats into the flour until the mixture resembles fresh breadcrumbs.

Beat the egg in a bowl and stir in 4 tbsp cold water. Drizzle into the flour, stirring with a knife, until the pastry comes together. (It may not be necessary to use all the egg.)

Shape the pastry into two flat discs, using one-third of the pastry for one and two-thirds for the other. Chill until firm.

To make the mincemeat, combine all the ingredients in a saucepan, except for the butter and walnuts. Cook over a low heat until the sugar melts, then simmer for about 15 minutes until the juices have nearly evaporated. Stir in the butter and walnuts, and transfer to a clean, hot jar. Place a waxed paper disc over the surface and, when cool, store in the fridge.

Pre-heat the oven to 190°C, 375°F, Gas 5. Roll out the smaller pastry disc and use it to line a 20 cm (8 in) tart tin with greaseproof paper and baking beans. Bake blind for 15 to 20 minutes. Transfer to a wire rack to cool.

Meanwhile, thinly roll out the larger pastry disc to a 25 cm (10 in) circle and cut into 1 cm (½ in) wide strips. Starting with the middle strip, twist and overlap the strips to form a lattice on a baking sheet. If the pastry becomes too soft to work with, put the baking sheet with the pastry on it into the freezer for 2 to 3 minutes. When the lattice is complete, chill well, reserving the trimmings.

Fill the cooked pastry with the mincemeat, then brush the edges with a little of the beaten egg white and slide the latticed pastry on top. Cut out shapes from the pastry trimmings and place around edge of tart (see opposite). Brush with the remaining beaten egg white and sprinkle with the caster sugar. Bake for 20 minutes, until lightly browned. Serve warm with the brandy cream.

To make the brandy cream, place the cream in a bowl, sieve over the icing sugar. Whisk until the cream holds its shape. Fold in the brandy. Chill.

877 CALS PER PORTION • 53 G FAT PER PORTION • PREPARATION TIME: 40 MIN • COOKING TIME: 40 MIN • CAN BE MADE 2 WEEKS AHEAD • FREEZE-ABILITY: 1 MONTH BEFORE FINAL COOKING.

SERVES 8

PASTRY
340 g (12 oz) plain flour

1 scant tsp salt

2 tbsp caster sugar

85 g (3 oz) butter or hard margarine

85 g (3 oz) hard vegetable fat or lard

1 medium egg

Beaten egg white

1 tbsp caster sugar

MINCEMEAT
2 Golden Delicious apples, peeled, cored and cut into 5 mm (¼ in) chunks

255 g (9 oz) large stoned raisins, halved

170 g (6 oz) dark brown sugar

½ orange, finely chopped with rind

½ lemon, finely chopped with rind

100 ml (3½ fl oz) apple juice

2 tbsp brandy

½ tsp salt

1 tsp ground cinnamon

½ tsp ground nutmeg

¼ tsp ground cloves

55 g (2 oz) butter or margarine

140 g (5 oz) walnuts, chopped

BRANDY CREAM
290 ml (½ pt) whipping cream

2 tbsp icing sugar

2 tbsp brandy

Home-made mincemeat is so wonderful that you will never buy another jar.

APPLE-ALMOND KUCHEN

SERVES 8

170 g (6 oz) plain flour

55 g (2 oz) ground almonds

110 g (4 oz) cold butter, cut
into small pieces

4 tbsp caster sugar

Grated zest of 1 lemon

½ tsp baking powder

Pinch of salt

Ground cinnamon, to dust

Crème fraîche, to serve (optional)

FILLING

4 red dessert apples

85 g (3 oz) caster sugar

1 tsp ground cinnamon

2 egg yolks

½ tsp vanilla essence

150 ml (¼ pt) whipping cream

Pre-heat the oven to 200°C, 400°F, Gas 6. Place the flour, ground almonds, butter, sugar, lemon zest, baking powder and salt in a large bowl and rub until the mixture resembles breadcrumbs. Press into a 22 cm (9 in) flan tin or ceramic dish. Chill for 10 minutes.

To make the filling, core the apples, cut in half, then slice into 5 mm (¼ in) slices. Arrange the apples over the pastry.

Combine the sugar and cinnamon in a bowl. Sprinkle over the apples.

Stir the egg yolks and vanilla essence into the cream, then pour over the apples.

Bake for 45 minutes, or until the custard is firm and the apples are lightly browned. Dust with ground cinnamon and serve warm with crème fraîche, if desired.

425 CALS PER PORTION • 26 G FAT PER PORTION • PREPARATION TIME: 40 MIN • COOKING TIME: 35–45 MIN • CAN BE MADE 1 WEEK AHEAD • FREEZE-ABILITY: 1 MONTH.

Of German origin, this delicious moist cake can be frozen. Defrost and warm in a 150°C, 300°F, Gas 2 oven for 15 minutes before serving.

RHUBARB AND BLUEBERRY STRUDEL

Pre-heat the oven to 200°C, 400°F, Gas 6. Combine the caster sugar, cornflour, cinnamon and breadcrumbs, then toss with the rhubarb and blueberries.

Lay two sheets of filo pastry on a clean work surface with the long edges slightly overlapping. Brush with a little of the melted butter. Place two more pastry sheets over the top and brush with more butter. Place two more pastry sheets over the top to make a total of three layers, about 25 x 45 cm (10 x 18 in).

Arrange the fruit mixture in a log shape along the edge of the pastry, leaving a 2.5 cm (1 in) border at each end. Fold over the edges of the pastry to keep the fruit from falling out. Carefully roll up the strudel, then place it on a large baking sheet, seam-side down. If the strudel is too long to fit on the baking sheet, curve it into a horse-shoe shape. Brush over the strudel with the remaining melted butter. If making ahead, store in the fridge at this point.

Bake the strudel in the top third of the oven for 20 to 25 minutes until golden brown.

Mix 1 tbsp of icing sugar with 2 tsp cold water in a small cup and brush over the top of the strudel. Return to the oven and continue to cook for 5 minutes. Dust with the remaining icing sugar and serve.

371 CALS PER PORTION • 6 G FAT PER PORTION • PREPARATION TIME: 15 MIN • COOKING TIME: 25-30 MIN • CAN BE MADE A DAY AHEAD • FREEZE-ABILITY: 1 MONTH.

SERVES 6

8 tbsp caster sugar

3 tbsp cornflour

½ tsp ground cinnamon

8 tbsp fresh white breadcrumbs

560 g (1¼ lb) trimmed rhubarb, cut into chunks

200 g (7 oz) blueberries, washed

200 g (7 oz) filo pastry

30 g (1 oz) unsalted butter, melted

2 tbsp icing sugar

Baking the rhubarb in filo pastry preserves its colour and texture. When rhubarb isn't in season, substitute with cooking apples.

STRAWBERRY AND MASCARPONE TART

Sieve the flour with the salt on to a piece of greaseproof paper.

Using a food processor, electric mixer or by hand cream together the butter, egg yolks, sugar and vanilla essence, then quickly mix in the flour. Shape the pastry into a flat round and wrap in clingfilm. Chill for 15 minutes, then roll between two sheets of clingfilm, to fit a 20 cm (8 in) tart tin. Line the tin with the pastry and chill until firm.

Pre-heat the oven to 190°C, 375°F, Gas 5. Line the pastry case with greaseproof paper, and fill with enough baking beans to support the sides of the pastry and just cover the base. Bake in the top third of the oven for 15 minutes, then remove the beans and continue to bake until completely cooked. The edges of the pastry may need protecting with foil, as they burn easily and should only be pale gold when cooked. Cool on a wire rack.

To make the filling, beat the mascarpone, then stir in the yoghurt and vanilla essence. Spread the mixture over the base of the pastry case.

Wash, hull and dry the strawberries, then arrange in the pastry case. To make the glaze, melt the redcurrant jelly over a low heat, then pass through a fine sieve. Generously brush over the strawberries.

441 CALS PER PORTION • 27 G FAT PER PORTION • PREPARATION TIME: 30 MIN • COOKING TIME: 25 MIN • CAN BE MADE A DAY AHEAD • FREEZE-ABILITY: PASTRY ONLY, 1 MONTH.

SERVES 8

170 g (6 oz) plain flour
Pinch of salt
85 g (3 oz) butter, softened
3 egg yolks
85 g (3 oz) caster sugar
2 drops of vanilla essence
FILLING
255 g (9 oz) mascarpone cheese
90 ml (3 fl oz) Greek yoghurt
2 drops of vanilla essence
2 punnets of strawberries
170 g (6 oz) redcurrant jelly

Strawberries and mascarpone make a particularly delicious combination with the crisp, biscuit pastry.

CHOCOLATE AND CINNAMON TART

SERVES 8

110 g (4 oz) plain flour

30 g (1 oz) cocoa powder

Pinch of salt

85 g (3 oz) butter

2 tbsp caster sugar

1 egg yolk

Icing sugar, to dust

Coffee beans, to decorate

FILLING

200g (7 oz) plain chocolate

55 g (2 oz) unsalted butter

3 eggs

55 g (2 oz) golden caster sugar

120 ml (4 fl oz) double cream

30 g (1 oz) cocoa powder

1 tsp ground cinnamon

½ tsp vanilla essence

The cinnamon mellows the chocolate without being too noticeable in this fudgy tart.

Sieve the flour, cocoa powder and salt into a bowl or food processor. Cut in the butter until the mixture resembles breadcrumbs, then add the sugar. Mix the egg yolk with 2 tbsp cold water and drizzle over the flour mixture. Stir together.

On a lightly floured surface, roll out the pastry and use it to line a 20 cm (8 in) flan ring. Chill until firm.

Pre-heat the oven to 190°C, 375°F, Gas 5. Line the pastry case with greaseproof paper, support the sides with baking beans and bake for 10 minutes. Remove the beans and bake for a further 10 minutes. Cool on a wire rack. Reduce the oven temperature to 180°C, 350°F, Gas 4.

To make the filling, melt the chocolate with the butter over simmering water. Remove from the heat and cool slightly. Stir the eggs, sugar and cream into the mixture, sieve the cocoa and cinnamon over and fold in. Stir in the vanilla essence.

Pour the mixture into the pastry case and bake for 30 minutes. Allow to cool. Dust with the icing sugar, decorate with coffee beans. Serve with Coffee Bean Sauce (see recipe opposite).

447 CALS PER PORTION • 33 G FAT PER PORTION • PREPARATION TIME: 30 MIN • COOKING TIME: 30 MIN • CAN BE MADE 3 DAYS AHEAD • FREEZE-ABILITY: 1 MONTH.

COFFEE BEAN SAUCE

Place the coffee beans in a plastic bag and bash with a rolling pin to roughly crush. Combine with the milk and cream in a small pan then heat until steaming. Allow to infuse for 10 minutes.

Combine the egg yolks and sugar, then pour the coffee mixture slowly on to the egg mixture, stirring to form a custard.

Place the custard in a small pan over a medium heat and stir until the mixture thickens. Stir in the vanilla essence.

Pour into a cold bowl. Place greaseproof paper on the surface of the custard if it is not needed immediately. Allow to cool then store in the fridge for up to one day.

92 CALS PER PORTION • 7 G FAT PER PORTION • PREPARATION TIME: 5 MIN • COOKING TIME: 5 MIN •
CAN BE MADE A DAY AHEAD • FREEZE-ABILITY: CANNOT BE FROZEN.

SERVES 8

1 tbsp whole roasted coffee beans

150 ml ($\frac{1}{4}$ pt) milk

150 ml ($\frac{1}{4}$ pt) single cream

3 egg yolks, beaten

30 g (1 oz) caster sugar

$\frac{1}{2}$ tsp vanilla essence

This delicious coffee custard complements the Chocolate and Cinnamon Tart perfectly (see recipe opposite).

ANGEL ROSE CAKE

WITH SUMMER BERRY SAUCE

SERVES 10

8 medium egg whites

Pinch of salt

1 tsp cream of tartar

255 g (9 oz) caster sugar

$\frac{1}{2}$ tsp almond essence

$\frac{1}{2}$ tsp rose water

140 g (5 oz) plain flour

SAUCE

1 kg (2$\frac{1}{4}$ lb) mixed soft fruit

55 g (2 oz) caster sugar

1 tsp rose water

Pre-heat the oven to 170°C, 320°F, Gas 3. Beat the egg whites in a clean, dry bowl with the salt and cream of tartar until just stiff. As you beat the whites, slowly add the sugar in a continual stream – this should take about 1 minute.

Pour the almond essence and rose water around the edge of mixture, then sieve in half the flour and gently fold into the mixture. Sieve the remaining flour over the mixture and fold in until combined.

Carefully turn the mixture into a 25 cm (10 in) tube pan or 20 cm (8 in) round loose-bottomed cake tin and immediately place in the centre of the oven for 40 to 50 minutes or until well risen and browned – a wooden skewer inserted into the middle should come out clean.

Allow the cake to cool in the tin. Release the edges of the cake with a thin knife to remove it from the tin.

To make the sauce, purée 200g (7 oz) of fruit with the sugar and rose water. Stir the sauce into the remaining fruit and chill until required. To serve, cut the cake into slices and surround with the sauce.

206 CALS PER PORTION • 0.5 G FAT PER PORTION • PREPARATION TIME: 5 MIN • COOKING TIME: 40–50 MIN • CAN BE MADE 3 DAYS AHEAD • FREEZE-ABILITY: 1 MONTH.

This American fat-free cake is traditionally made in a 25 cm (10 in) tube pan, although a 20 cm (8 in) round loose-bottomed cake tin can be used. Make sure the tin and all utensils are clean and grease-free.

CHAPTER THIRTEEN

ICE CREAMS AND SORBETS

SUMMER BERRY SORBET

SERVES 6

225 g (8 oz) granulated sugar

Pared zest and juice of 1 lemon

225 g (8 oz) mixed summer fruit, such as raspberries, strawberries and blackcurrants

1 egg white

Mint sprigs, to decorate

The summer fruit flavours sing in this refreshing ice. Use frozen fruit when summer fruit is hard to find. Remember, uncooked egg should not be served to pregnant women, the very young or the very old.

Place the sugar in a saucepan with 540 ml (18 fl oz) water and the pared zest and juice of the lemon. Heat over a low heat until the sugar dissolves then turn up the heat and boil for 5 minutes. Leave the syrup to cool.

Purée the fruit in a liquidiser or food processor then push it through a sieve to remove any seeds. There should be 225 ml (8 fl oz) of purée.

Remove the lemon zest from the syrup then stir the syrup into the fruit purée.

Freeze the sorbet mixture in an ice cream machine, according to the manufacturer's directions, adding the egg white at the end of churning. Freeze until required.

If you don't have an ice cream machine, pour the sorbet mixture into a rigid container and freeze until solid. Remove from the freezer and leave to stand for 20 minutes at room temperature. Cut the sorbet into chunks and blend in a food processor until just smooth. Add the egg white when the motor is running and process for 30 seconds. Return to the freezer until required.

About 30 minutes before serving, take the sorbet out of the freezer and place it in the fridge to soften slightly. Decorate with mint sprigs and serve.

162 CALS PER PORTION • 0 G FAT PER PORTION • PREPARATION TIME: 15 MIN • COOKING TIME: 20 MIN • CAN BE MADE 1 WEEK AHEAD • FREEZE-ABILITY: 1 WEEK.

TOASTED ALMOND BISCOTTI

Pre-heat the oven to 180°C, 350°F, Gas 4. Line a baking sheet with silicon paper.

In a large mixing bowl, beat together the eggs, grated orange zest, caster sugar, vanilla essence and almond essence. Sift all the dry ingredients, except the almonds, over the egg mixture, and stir until combined. Work in the almonds.

Divide the dough into two equal-sized logs, about 25 x 7 cm (12 x 3 in) on the prepared baking tray. Use a little flour on your hands if the dough is very sticky. Bake in the oven for 20 minutes or until the logs are golden brown and slightly risen.

Leave to stand on a wire rack for 10 minutes then slice at an angle into biscuits about 1 cm (½ in) wide. Place the biscuits on their side on the baking tray and return to the oven for about 15 minutes. Turn the biscuits over and continue to bake for 5 minutes. Leave to cool on a wire rack and store in an airtight container.

91 CALS PER PORTION • 3 G FAT PER PORTION • PREPARATION TIME: 15 MIN • COOKING TIME: 50 MIN • CAN BE MADE 2 WEEKS AHEAD • FREEZE-ABILITY: 3 MONTHS.

MAKES ABOUT 30

125 g (4 oz) whole blanched almonds, toasted
2 medium eggs
Grated zest of 1 orange
140 g (5 oz) caster sugar
½ tsp vanilla essence
¼ tsp almond essence
170 g (6 oz) plain flour
55 g (2 oz) polenta
¼ tsp salt
½ tsp bicarbonate of soda
Flour for shaping

These crunchy biscuits are ideal with the Summer Berry Sorbet (see recipe opposite) or served with after-dinner coffee.

HOT CHILLI PINEAPPLE

AND COCONUT ICE CREAM

For the ice cream, put the milk in a pan with the vanilla pod, heat until steaming, then leave to infuse for 15 minutes. Remove the pod, scrape out the seeds and add to the milk.

Mix together the egg yolks and sugar, then slowly add the milk, stirring. Return the mixture to the pan.

Stir in the coconut milk powder and heat until the mixture is thick enough to coat the back of a spoon (do not boil). Sieve, and set aside to cool.

If using an ice-cream machine, stir in the cream and cooled mixture and churn according to the manufacturer's instructions. If freezing without a machine, put the custard base in the freezer until half frozen, then beat with a fork to break up the ice crystals. Whip the cream until soft peaks form, then beat it into the custard base. Freeze until firm.

About 20 minutes before serving, remove the ice cream from the freezer to soften slightly. Sprinkle the pineapple with the diced chillies, reserving some for decoration.

Heat the butter in a pan over a medium heat and fry the pineapple for 3 minutes on each side until lightly browned. Add the Malibu liqueur and quickly light it with a match to flame, taking care to stand back. Stir in the orange zest and juice.

Arrange the pineapple on individual plates and spoon over the juice. Top with the coconut ice cream and decorate with the reserved diced chillies.

321 CALS PER PORTION • 21 G FAT PER PORTION • PREPARATION TIME: 40 MIN • COOKING TIME: 5 MIN • PINEAPPLE CAN BE MADE A DAY AHEAD • FREEZE-ABILITY: ICE CREAM, 1 WEEK.

SERVES 8

290 ml (½ pt) milk

1 vanilla pod

3 egg yolks, beaten

85 g (3 oz) caster sugar

8 tbsp coconut milk powder

290 ml (½ pt) whipping cream

CHILLI PINEAPPLE

1 large ripe pineapple, peeled, cored
   and sliced

2 green chillies, de-seeded and
   finely diced

30 g (1 oz) butter

60 ml (2 fl oz) Malibu liqueur

Grated zest and juice of 1 orange

Striking contrasts of hot and cold, sweet and spicy, make this dessert particularly enticing. A perfect finish to an Asian-inspired meal.

FROZEN LIME MOUSSE WITH

BLACKBERRY COULIS

SERVES 6

Oil for greasing

400 g (14 oz) canned sweetened
condensed milk

Zest and juice of 4 limes

Zest and juice of 1 lemon

3 medium egg whites

40 g (1½ oz) butter, melted and cooled

85 g (3 oz) digestive biscuits, crushed

BLACKBERRY COULIS

140 g (5 oz) caster sugar

255 g (9 oz) fresh blackberries

Mint sprigs and julienne strips of
lime, to decorate

This is a deliciously cool finish
to a spicy meal. Remember it
is not recommended to serve
uncooked eggs to those who
are young, old or pregnant.

Lightly grease six 150 ml (¼ pt) timbale moulds or ramekins and line with clingfilm. Beat together the condensed milk and the zest and juices of the limes and lemon until thick and pale.

Whisk the egg whites in a large bowl until just stiff, then fold into the condensed milk mixture in two additions. Carefully turn the mixture into the prepared moulds or ramekins.

Combine the melted butter with the crushed digestive biscuits in a bowl, then sprinkle over the top of the mousse mixture and pat gently. Cover with clingfilm and freeze for at least 4 hours or up to a week.

To make the blackberry coulis, place the caster sugar and 150 ml (¼ pt) water in a small saucepan over a low heat. When the sugar has dissolved, bring to the boil for 1 minute. Reserving a few of the blackberries for decoration, add the remainder to the pan and cook for 1 minute. Push the sauce through a sieve to remove any seeds. Store in the fridge for up to 1 week.

About 30 minutes before serving, transfer the mousses to the fridge to soften slightly. Carefully unmould on to individual plates and decorate with the reserved blackberries, mint sprigs and lime strips. Serve with the blackberry coulis.

451 CALS PER PORTION • 16 G FAT PER PORTION • PREPARATION TIME: 25 MIN • COOKING TIME: 5 MIN •
CAN BE MADE 1 WEEK AHEAD • FREEZE-ABILITY: MUST BE FROZEN FOR 4 HR OR UP TO 1 WEEK.

PLUM, PEAR AND GINGER SORBET

Put the sugar in a saucepan, add 570 ml (1 pt) water, the ginger and lemon zest and juice. Stir over a low heat until the sugar dissolves and then turn up the heat and boil for 5 minutes. Halve and stone the plums, peel, quarter and remove the cores of the pears, then add both fruits to the syrup.

Poach the fruit until it is tender and the pears are translucent. Leave to cool and then discard the lemon zest and ginger. Purée the fruit and syrup in a food processor and put through a sieve.

If you have an ice-cream machine, freeze the fruit purée according to the manufacturer's instructions. Otherwise, freeze it in a container for about 2 hours, then beat with a fork and return to the freezer for another 1 hour until it is nearly solid.

Now whisk the egg whites until just stiff and fold into the fruit mixture. Churn in the ice-cream machine or blend briefly in a blender to combine. Return to the freezer until required.

Scoop the sorbet into glass dessert dishes and garnish with mint sprigs.

256 CALS PER PORTION • 0.10 G FAT PER PORTION • PREPARATION TIME: 15 MIN • COOKING TIME: 25 MIN •
CAN BE MADE 1 WEEK AHEAD • FREEZE-ABILITY: 1 WEEK.

SERVES 6

450 g (1 lb) granulated sugar

5 cm (2 in) piece of ginger, peeled and sliced

Pared zest and juice of 1 lemon

340 g (12 oz) red plums

340 g (12 oz) pears

2 egg whites

6 to 8 sprigs of mint, to decorate

A light, refreshing ice with no cream – the perfect finish to a rich meal.

The deep red juice from blood oranges makes a vibrant sorbet.

SANGUINELLO SORBET

SERVES 6

285 g (10 oz) granulated sugar
Juice of 1 lemon
425 ml (¾ pt) Sanguinello
(blood orange) juice
Raspberries, and mint sprigs, to decorate

Place the sugar in a saucepan and cover with 340 ml (12 fl oz) water and the lemon juice. Place over a low heat until the sugar dissolves, then bring to the boil for 2 minutes. Add the orange juice and leave to cool completely.

Freeze the sorbet mixture in an ice cream machine according to the manufacturer's directions. If you do not have a machine, freeze it in a shallow container, stirring with a fork to break up ice crystals every 45 minutes until frozen.

About 30 minutes before serving, take the sorbet out of the freezer and place the sorbet in the fridge to soften slightly. Serve each portion in a Chocolate Lace Basket with Raspberry Coulis (see recipes opposite). Decorate with raspberries and mint sprigs.

221 CALS PER PORTION • 0 G FAT PER PORTION • PREPARATION TIME: 15 MIN • COOKING TIME: 25 MIN •
CAN BE MADE 1 WEEK AHEAD • FREEZE-ABILITY: 1 WEEK.

CHOCOLATE LACE BASKETS

Line a baking sheet with silicon paper.

Pre-heat the oven to 190°C, 375°F, Gas 5. Place the butter, syrup and sugar in a small saucepan and heat until the butter has melted. Remove the pan from the heat and leave the mixture to cool, but do not allow it to harden.

Sieve in the flour and cocoa powder, then stir in the brandy. Place tablespoonfuls of the mixture on the baking sheet, allowing room for the mixture to spread, and flatten with dampened fingers.

Bake 2 tbsp at a time in the oven for about 7 to 8 minutes or until lacy and slightly browned around the edges. Leave to cool slightly until just pliable, then drape them over upturned ramekins. If they are misshapen, they can be trimmed with scissors while still warm. If they become too cold, they will be brittle and impossible to shape – return to the oven for 1 minute to make them pliable again.

Leave the biscuits to cool completely, then store in an airtight container until required.

139 CALS PER PORTION • 6 G FAT PER PORTION • PREPARATION TIME: 30 MIN • COOKING TIME: 8 MIN • CAN BE MADE 2 WEEKS AHEAD • FREEZE-ABILITY: NOT ADVISABLE.

MAKES 8

55 g (2 oz) butter
4 tbsp golden syrup
55 g (2 oz) caster sugar
70 g (2½ oz) plain flour
15 g (½ oz) cocoa powder
1 tsp brandy

Although tricky to make, these brandy-snap-type baskets look impressive.

RASPBERRY COULIS

Place the sugar in a small saucepan and cover with 290 ml (½ pt) water. Cook over a low heat until the sugar dissolves, then turn up the heat and boil for 2 minutes.

Add the raspberries to the syrup and boil for 1 minute.

Push the mixture through a sieve to remove any seeds, then adjust the taste with the lemon juice. Chill until required.

104 CALS PER PORTION • 0 G FAT PER PORTION • PREPARATION TIME: 10 MIN • COOKING TIME: 5 MIN • CAN BE MADE 1 WEEK AHEAD • FREEZE-ABILITY: 1 MONTH.

SERVES 6

140 g (5 oz) granulated sugar
300 g (10 oz) raspberries
Lemon juice to taste

Add colour and flavour to desserts with this classic coulis.

GINGER MERINGUE BOMBE

SERVES 8

55 g (2 oz) whole blanched almonds
2 medium egg whites
110 g (4 oz) golden caster sugar
BOMBE
570 ml (1 pt) double cream
3 tbsp brandy
4 pieces of chopped preserved stem ginger
2 tbsp syrup from preserved stem ginger jar
Icing sugar to taste

Serve this delicious dessert with
Hot Chocolate Sauce
for a refreshing finish to an
elaborate meal.

Pre-heat the oven to 180°C, 350°F, Gas 4. Toast the almonds for 8 minutes. Cool, then crush in a grinder or food processor.

Reduce the oven temperature to 130°C, 250°F, Gas 1. Line a baking sheet with silicon paper. Whisk the egg whites until just stiff. Add the sugar, 1 tsp at a time, whisking between each addition. When half the sugar has been added, fold in the rest.

Fold in the ground almonds. Place the meringue in 8 mounds on the prepared baking sheet and bake for 1½ hours or until dry. Cool and break into 2.5 cm (1 in) pieces.

To make the bombe, whip the cream until it holds its shape, then fold in the brandy, stem ginger pieces, syrup and meringue pieces. Sweeten with a little sifted icing sugar, if desired. Spoon into a bombe mould or freezerproof bowl and put into the freezer immediately. Freeze overnight.

When required, turn the bombe out on to a serving plate and leave to stand in the fridge for 20 minutes before serving. Pour over the Hot Chocolate Sauce (see recipe below).

442 CALS PER PORTION • 38 G FAT PER PORTION • PREPARATION TIME: 30 MIN • COOKING TIME: 1½ HR • CAN BE MADE 1 MONTH AHEAD • FREEZE-ABILITY: 1 MONTH.

HOT CHOCOLATE SAUCE

SERVES 8

110 g (4 oz) plain dark chocolate
30 g (1 oz) butter
170 g (6 oz) golden caster sugar
2 tbsp golden syrup
1 tsp vanilla essence

This sauce becomes deliciously
fudgy when poured
over ice cream.

Break the chocolate into pieces and melt with the butter in a bowl over a saucepan of simmering water.

Melt the caster sugar and golden syrup in 240 ml (8 fl oz) water over a low heat until dissolved. Stir in the melted chocolate.

Boil the mixture, stirring continuously, for exactly 5 minutes.

Remove the pan from the heat, leave to cool slightly, then stir in the vanilla essence.

Serve the chocolate sauce warm over the Ginger Meringue Bombe (see recipe above) or vanilla ice cream.

196 CALS PER PORTION • 7 G FAT PER PORTION • PREPARATION TIME: 5 MIN • COOKING TIME: 5 MIN • CAN BE MADE 1 WEEK AHEAD • FREEZE-ABILITY: NOT ADVISABLE.

WHITE CHOCOLATE PARFAIT
WITH PASSION FRUIT SAUCE

Lightly oil a 1.2 ltr (2 pt) loaf tin and line with clingfilm.

Place the chocolate and 150 ml (¼ pt) of cream in a bowl over a saucepan of simmering water, making sure the base of the bowl does not touch the water in the pan. Melt the chocolate, stirring occasionally, then remove from the heat.

Place the sugar, vanilla pod and 60 ml (2 fl oz) water in a small saucepan over a low heat until the sugar dissolves. Boil the syrup until it reaches soft ball stage on a sugar thermometer (about 115°C, 238°F).

Meanwhile, whisk the egg whites until soft peaks form. When the syrup reaches the correct temperature, remove the vanilla pod and pour the syrup on to the egg whites. Continue to whisk for about 2 minutes, or until the mixture forms stiff peaks.

Split the vanilla pod lengthways and scrape out the tiny seeds. Stir the seeds into the melted chocolate, along with the lemon juice, reserving the vanilla pod for decoration.

Fold a large spoonful of the egg whites into the chocolate to loosen it, then fold in the remaining whites.

Whip the remaining cream until soft peaks form and fold into the chocolate mixture. Turn into the prepared tin, smooth the surface and freeze for at least 4 hours.

To make the passion fruit sauce, peel the mangoes and place the flesh in a processor with the passion fruit seeds and pulp and the orange juice. Purée until smooth (the seeds can be sieved out first, if preferred). Do not use a liquidiser as it will pulverise the seeds.

About 30 minutes before serving, remove the parfait from the freezer and place in the fridge to soften slightly. Turn out on to a board and cut into slices. Serve with the sauce.

429 CALS PER PORTION • 31 G FAT PER PORTION • PREPARATION TIME: 30 MIN •
CAN BE MADE 1 WEEK AHEAD • FREEZE-ABILITY: 1 WEEK.

SERVES 8

255 g (9 oz) good-quality white
   chocolate, chopped
425 ml (¾ pt) whipping cream
85 g (3 oz) granulated sugar
4 large egg whites
2 tsp fresh lemon juice
PASSION FRUIT SAUCE
2 ripe mangoes
2 ripe passion fruit
Juice of 1 orange

This is a velvety ice cream complemented by a tangy sauce.

OVERLEAF • WHITE CHOCOLATE PARFAIT WITH PASSION FRUIT SAUCE

CHAPTER FOURTEEN
BREADS

THREE-SEED ROLLS

MAKES 14 ROLLS

15 g (½ oz) fresh yeast or 2 tsp
dried yeast

1 tsp caster sugar

225 g (8 oz) strong white flour

225 g (8 oz) strong wholemeal flour

2 tsp salt

2 tbsp olive oil

Oil for greasing

6 tbsp mixed seeds, such as poppy,
sesame, millet and sunflower

Beaten egg for glazing

Vary the seeds as you like –
they give the rolls a wonderful
nutty flavour and lots of
texture. The rolls freeze
beautifully so make extra.

Cream the yeast with the sugar and a little warm water. If using dried yeast, allow the mixture to stand for 10 minutes, or until it becomes foamy.

Sieve the flours and salt into a large bowl and make a well in the centre. Add the yeast mixture to the well, along with the oil and about 290 ml (½ pt) warm water to make a soft dough. Knead the dough for about 8 to 10 minutes, or until smooth and elastic.

Place the dough in a large oiled bowl, turning it so it is coated with a thin film of oil. Cover with clingfilm and leave in a warm place to rise for about 1 hour, or until doubled in size.

Pre-heat the oven to 220°C, 425°F, Gas 7.

Knock back the dough by pushing it down and pulling the edges into the centre. Knead for 30 seconds, then roll out on a floured surface to about 2.5 cm (1 in) thick. Reserving 2 tbsp of seeds, sprinkle the remainder over the dough. Fold the dough over itself to encase the seeds and continue to knead for 10 seconds.

Shape the dough into 14 equal-sized rounds or two loaf shapes and place on oiled baking sheets or in lightly oiled loaf tins. Cover with oiled clingfilm and leave in a warm place to prove until one-and-a-half times its original size.

Glaze with the beaten egg, sprinkle with the reserved seeds and cook in the oven for 20 minutes for rolls, or 30 to 35 minutes for loaves. When done, the bread will feel light and sound hollow when tapped on the underside. Turn out of the tins and leave on a wire rack to cool.

To store, place in a plastic bag and leave in a cool, dry place for up to two days. To freeze, wrap tightly to exclude air and freeze for up to one month. Defrost at room temperature, then refresh by placing in an oven pre-heated to 180°C, 350°F, Gas 4 for 10 minutes.

155 CALS PER PORTION • 5 G FAT PER PORTION • PREPARATION TIME: 1¼ HR • COOKING TIME: 20–30 MIN • CAN BE MADE 2 DAYS AHEAD • FREEZE-ABILITY: 3 MONTHS.

FAN TAN ROLLS

Heat the milk until steaming, then set aside until lukewarm.

Mix the yeast with the sugar and a little of the milk to make a paste.

Sift the flour and salt into a bowl, then rub in the lard or vegetable shortening. Make a well in the centre, pour in the yeast mixture, remaining milk and egg. Stir to form a soft dough. Knead for 10 minutes until smooth but not sticky.

Place the dough in an oiled bowl and turn to coat with the oil. Cover with clingfilm and leave in a warm place to rise for about 1 hour until doubled in size.

Knead the dough for 1 minute to knock it back. Return it to the bowl for 45 minutes until doubled in size.

Knead the dough for 30 seconds, then roll it out until 5 mm (¼ in) thick. Trim to a 22 cm (9 in) wide rectangle.

Pre-heat the oven to 190°C, 375°F, Gas 5. Lightly butter 16 muffin cups. Spread the dough with the remaining butter and cut it lengthways into 6 strips. Stack the strips, then cut them into 4 cm (1½ in) square pieces. Place in muffin cups, cover with oiled clingfilm and leave in a warm place for 30 minutes.

Cook the rolls for 30 minutes until browned (they should sound hollow when tapped on the underside).

Before serving, reheat by placing in an oven pre-heated to 180°C, 350°F, Gas 4 for 10 minutes.

154 CALS PER PORTION • 6 G FAT PER PORTION • PREPARATION TIME: 30 MIN, PLUS RISING TIME •
COOKING TIME: 30 MIN • CAN BE MADE A DAY AHEAD • FREEZE-ABILITY: 1 MONTH.

MAKES 16

200 ml (7 fl oz) milk
15 g (½ oz) fresh yeast
2 tsp caster sugar
450 g (1 lb) strong white flour
2 tsp salt
30 g (1 oz) lard or vegetable shortening
1 medium egg, beaten
Oil for greasing
55 g (2 oz) butter, softened

The buttery layers of these rolls make them a favourite with my children.

ITALIAN OLIVE OIL BREAD

Dissolve the fresh yeast in a little warm water, or dissolve the dry yeast according to the packet instructions.

Sift the flour and salt into a large bowl, make a well in the centre, then add the yeast and 3 tbsp of olive oil. Stir in about 250 ml (9 fl oz) warm water to form a soft dough and knead for 10 minutes. Place in an oiled bowl and leave in a warm place for 10 minutes.

Pre-heat the oven to 220°C, 425°F, Gas 7. Sprinkle the polenta on to a baking sheet. Roll out the dough to a 20 x 40 cm (8 x 15 in) oval, then place on the baking sheet and cover closely with oiled clingfilm. Leave in a warm place to rise for 45 minutes until doubled in size.

Using your finger or the handle of a wooden spoon, make indentations about 5 cm (2 in) apart in the bread. Brush with the remaining oil, sprinkle with sea salt and garnish with rosemary leaves in the indentations. Leave to stand for a further 5 minutes.

Bake the bread in the top third of the oven for 15 minutes. Reduce the oven temperature to 190°C, 375°F, Gas 5, and continue to bake for 20 minutes until golden.

Before serving, reheat by placing in an oven pre-heated to 180°C, 350°F, Gas 4 for 10 minutes.

252 CALS PER PORTION • 6 G FAT PER PORTION • PREPARATION TIME: 20 MIN, PLUS 1 HR RISING •
COOKING TIME: 35 MIN • CAN BE MADE A DAY AHEAD • FREEZE-ABILITY: AFTER BAKING, 1 MONTH.

SERVES 8

30 g (1 oz) fresh yeast or 1 sachet of
  dried yeast
450 g (1 lb) strong flour
2 level tsp salt
4 tbsp olive oil
Oil for greasing
1 tbsp polenta
1 tbsp sea salt
2 rosemary sprigs

If you have never made bread before, this is the time to start. This recipe is very easy and the result will be loved by all.

SESAME BREAD STICKS

MAKES 15

1 tsp dried yeast or 7 g ($^{1}/_{4}$ oz) fresh yeast
Pinch of caster sugar
225 g (8 oz) strong white flour
1 tsp sea salt
3 tbsp olive oil
3 tbsp sesame seeds
1 egg white, beaten
Coarse sea salt, for sprinkling

*These breadsticks are easy to
make and very more-ish. The
recipe can easily be doubled
for hungry families.*

Stir the yeast and caster sugar into 150 ml (¼ pt) warm water. Allow to stand for 10 minutes.

Sieve the flour and salt into a large bowl and make a well in the centre. Pour the yeast mixture and oil into the well and stir to make a soft but not sticky dough.

Knead the dough for 10 minutes by hand or 5 minutes with a machine. Place in a lightly oiled bowl and cover with clingfilm. Leave in a warm place for about 1 hour to rise or until doubled in size.

Pre-heat the oven to 220°C, 425°F, Gas 7. Turn the dough out on to a work surface and knead in 2 tbsp of sesame seeds. Divide the dough into 15 equal-sized pieces, then roll into 30 cm (12 in) long sticks using your fingers.

Place the dough sticks on ungreased baking sheets. Brush with the egg white and sprinkle with the remaining sesame seeds and a little coarse sea salt.

Bake in the oven for about 15 to 20 minutes until golden brown and firm to the touch. Leave to cool on a wire rack, then store in an airtight container for up to 1 week.

91 CALS PER PORTION • 4 G FAT PER PORTION • PREPARATION TIME: 1 HR 20 MIN • COOKING TIME: 20 MIN •
CAN BE MADE 1 WEEK AHEAD • FREEZE-ABILITY: NOT ADVISABLE.

GRILLED FLAT BREAD

Mix the yeast and sugar with 150 ml (¼ pt) warm water and allow to stand for 10 minutes.

Sieve the flour and salt into a large bowl, then stir in the yeast mixture and oil to make a soft, but not sticky, dough.

Turn out the dough and knead for about 10 minutes by hand or 5 minutes by machine. Place in an oiled bowl and cover closely with oiled clingfilm. Stand the bowl in a warm place until the dough doubles in size.

Turn out the dough and knead for about 1 minute. Divide into eight balls. Roll each ball in the polenta, then flatten it into a round, about 12 cm (5 in) in diameter. The bread can be frozen at this point by brushing it with olive oil and then layering it between sheets of clingfilm. Defrost before baking.

Pre-heat the grill to high. Place the bread in a single layer on a greased baking sheet and grill on each side for 2 minutes, or until puffed and golden. Serve warm. (It can be cooked the day before and warmed before serving.)

To store, place in a plastic bag and leave in a cool, dry place for up to two days. To freeze, wrap tightly to exclude air and freeze for up to one month. Defrost at room temperature, then refresh by placing in an oven pre-heated to 180°C, 350°F, Gas 4 for 10 minutes.

153 CALS PER PORTION • 4 G FAT PER PORTION • PREPARATION TIME: 90 MIN • COOKING TIME: 5 MIN • CAN BE MADE A DAY AHEAD • FREEZE-ABILITY: 1 MONTH.

MAKES 8

1 tsp dried yeast or 15 g (½ oz) fresh yeast
1 tsp sugar
255 g (9 oz) strong unbleached white flour
1 tsp salt
2 tbsp olive oil
Oil for greasing
2 tbsp polenta
Olive oil for brushing

This flat bread is great with dips and grilled meats.

OVERLEAF • GRILLED FLAT BREAD

WHOLEMEAL REFRIGERATOR BREAD

MAKES 2 LOAVES OR 16 ROLLS

340 g (12 oz) strong white flour

3540 g (12 oz) strong stone-ground wholemeal flour

1 tbsp salt

30 g (1 oz) fresh yeast or 1 sachet easy-blend yeast

2 tbsp clear honey

30 g (1 oz) butter, melted and cooled

Oil for greasing

Pinch of saffron strands

2 egg yolks

2 tbsp poppy seeds (optional)

Leaving the dough to rise overnight in the fridge makes it easy to produce delicious fresh bread.

Sift both flours and the salt into a large bowl and stir in the yeast, then the honey, melted butter and 425–570 ml (¾–1 pt) warm water to make a soft but not sticky dough. Knead for 10 minutes, then turn the dough over in a lightly oiled bowl so that it is coated with a thin film of oil. Cover the bowl with lightly oiled clingfilm and leave overnight to rise in the fridge.

Next day, if you want to freeze the dough, knead it lightly for 2 minutes then store in the freezer in a lightly oiled freezer bag.

Otherwise, leave the dough to come to room temperature and pre-heat the oven to 200°C, 400°F, Gas 6.

Knead the dough for 2 minutes and shape in oiled loaf tins or as rolls on baking sheets. Cover with lightly oiled clingfilm and leave in a warm place to rise until doubled in size.

Crush the saffron strands in 1 tsp hot water, beat this into the egg yolks and carefully brush the glaze over the rolls or tops of the loaves. Sprinkle with the poppy seeds if using, and bake on the top shelf of the oven for about 20 minutes for rolls and 30 minutes for loaves. When they are done they will be well-browned and hollow-sounding when tapped on the underside (turn loaves out of their tins to test this).

To store, place in a plastic bag and leave in a cool, dry place for up to two days. To freeze, wrap tightly to exclude air and freeze for up to one month. Defrost at room temperature, then refresh by placing in an oven pre-heated to 180°C, 350°F, Gas 4 for 10 minutes.

184 CALS PER PORTION • 4 G FAT PER PORTION • PREPARATION TIME: 25 MIN PLUS OVERNIGHT RISING • COOKING TIME: 30 MIN • DOUGH IS MADE A DAY AHEAD • FREEZE-ABILITY: DOUGH OR FINISHED LOAVES. 1 MONTH.

PREVIOUS PAGE • WHOLEMEAL REFRIGERATOR BREAD

PARMESAN AND CHIVE SCONES

Pre-heat the oven to 220°C, 425°F, Gas 7. Flour a baking sheet.

Sift the flour, salt, bicarbonate of soda and cream of tartar into a large bowl.

Cut the butter into small pieces and rub it into the flour with your fingertips until the mixture resembles breadcrumbs, then stir in the Parmesan and chives.

Make a well in the mixture, pour in the buttermilk and quickly mix to a soft dough using a table knife. Knead lightly on a floured surface until smooth.

Roll out the dough until 2.5 cm (1 in) thick and cut into rounds using a small floured scone-cutter. Place the rounds on the floured baking sheet, brush the tops with the beaten egg and bake on the top shelf of the oven for 12 to 14 minutes or until risen and browned. Serve warm. To reheat, wrap in foil and place in an oven pre-heated to 180°C, 350°F, Gas 4 for 10 minutes.

Before serving, warm by placing in an oven pre-heated to 180°C, 350°F, Gas 4 for 10 minutes.

210 CALS PER PORTION • 7 G FAT PER PORTION • PREPARATION TIME: 10 MIN • COOKING TIME: 15 MIN • CAN BE MADE 6 HR AHEAD • FREEZE-ABILITY: 3 MONTHS.

MAKES 12

225 g (8 oz) plain flour
1/2 tsp salt
1/2 tsp bicarbonate of soda
1/2 tsp cream of tartar
30 g (1 oz) butter
30 g (1 oz) Parmesan cheese, finely grated
1 tbsp finely chopped fresh chives
150 ml (1/4 pt) buttermilk
1 beaten egg to glaze

These scones make a good accompaniment to soups. If you can't get hold of buttermilk, use the equivalent quantity of regular milk, but substitute self-raising flour for the plain flour and 1 tsp baking powder for the bicarbonate of soda and cream of tartar.

CHEDDAR MUFFINS

Pre-heat the oven to 190°C, 375°F, Gas 5. Lightly butter 12 muffin tins.

Sift the flours, polenta, salt, baking powder, bicarbonate of soda and mustard into a bowl. Stir in the caraway seeds. Mix together the egg, oil and milk in a separate bowl and stir in all but 4 tbsp of cheese.

Make a well in the centre of the flour mixture, pour in milk mixture and stir quickly to make a batter. Pour into the tins. Sprinkle the reserved cheese over the top. Bake for 20 minutes until the muffins are well risen and golden. Cool for 5 minutes, remove from the tins and transfer to a wire rack to cool completely.

To store, place in a plastic bag and leave in a cool, dry place for up to two days. To freeze, wrap tightly to exclude air and freeze for up to one month. Defrost at room temperature, then refresh by placing in an oven pre-heated to 180°C, 350°F, Gas 4 for 10 minutes.

147 CALS PER PORTION • 8 G FAT PER PORTION • PREPARATION TIME: 10 MIN • COOKING TIME: 20 MIN •
CAN BE MADE 6 HR AHEAD • FREEZE-ABILITY: 1 MONTH.

MAKES 12

Butter for greasing

110 g (4 oz) plain flour

30 g (1 oz) wholewheat flour

85 g (3 oz) polenta

½ rounded tsp salt

1 tbsp baking powder

¼ tsp bicarbonate of soda

¼ tsp dry mustard

1 tsp caraway seeds

1 medium egg, beaten

4 tbsp vegetable oil

240 ml (8 fl oz) milk

85 g (3 oz) Cheddar cheese, finely grated

Wholesome and delicious, these muffins are a tasty alternative to bread rolls.

RED ONION FOCACCIA

MAKES 1 LOAF, CUT INTO
8 PORTIONS

450 g (1 lb) strong flour
2 tsp sea salt
30 g (1 oz) fresh yeast or 1 tbsp
dried yeast
4 tbsp olive oil
TOPPING
2 tbsp olive oil
285 g (10 oz) red onions
2 cloves garlic, peeled and crushed
1 tsp sea salt

This is a delicious
accompaniment
to an al fresco meal.

Sift the flour into a large bowl with the salt. Make a well in the centre.

Place the yeast in a small bowl and stir in a little warm water until dissolved. Allow to stand for 10 minutes. Add the yeast to the flour, along with the oil and about 340 ml (12 fl oz) warm water to make a soft but not sticky dough.

Turn the dough on to a lightly floured surface and knead for 10 minutes by hand or 5 minutes by machine. Transfer the dough to a lightly oiled bowl, turning it so it is coated in the oil. Cover with clingfilm and leave in a warm place to rise for about 1 hour until doubled in size.

Knead the dough again for 2 minutes, then press into a 30 x 25 cm (12 x 10 in) roasting tin lined with greaseproof paper. If making the focaccia in advance, cover the dough with oiled clingfilm and leave to chill overnight .

Otherwise leave the dough at room temperature until almost doubled in size. Meanwhile, pre-heat the oven to 200°C, 400°F, Gas 6.

To make the topping, place the oil in a sauté pan, stir in the onions and cover them with a piece of damp greaseproof paper. Cook over a low heat for 10 minutes. Remove the paper, stir in the garlic and sea salt and continue to cook for 1 minute. Turn on to a plate to cool.

Top the bread with the cooled onions and bake in the top third of the oven for 35 minutes, until golden brown.

Before serving, warm by placing in an oven pre-heated to 180°C, 350°F, Gas 4 for 10 minutes.

282 CALS PER PORTION • 9 G FAT PER PORTION • PREPARATION TIME: 20 MIN, PLUS 1 HR RISING/OVERNIGHT STORAGE • COOKING TIME: 35 MIN • CAN BE MADE A DAY AHEAD • FREEZE-ABILITY: 1 MONTH.

QUICK CHILLI BREAD

Pre-heat the oven to 180°C, 350°F, Gas 4. Line the base of a 20 x 10 x 6 cm (8 x 4 x 2½ in) loaf tin with greaseproof paper, then lightly oil the base and sides.

Wearing gloves, split the chillies lengthways, scrape away the seeds with a sharp knife. Chop the chillies and mix them with the dry ingredients and 3 tbsp Parmesan.

Mix the egg with the oil, soured cream and milk and stir into the dry ingredients. Turn the dough into the prepared tin, sprinkle with the remaining Parmesan and bake in the centre of the oven for about 55 minutes or until well risen and lightly browned. Let the bread stand in the tin for 5 minutes, then turn it out on to a wire rack to cool for a further 20 minutes.

Before serving, warm by placing in an oven pre-heated to 180°C, 350°F, Gas 4 for 10 minutes.

280 CALS PER PORTION • 13 G FAT PER PORTION • PREPARATION TIME: 10 MIN • COOKING TIME: 55 MIN • CAN BE MADE A DAY AHEAD • FREEZE-ABILITY: 1 MONTH.

SERVES 8

Oil for greasing

1 red and 1 green chilli

110 g (4 oz) polenta

225 g (8 oz) plain flour

1 tbsp baking powder

1 tbsp caster sugar

½ rounded tsp salt

4 tbsp freshly grated Parmesan cheese

1 medium egg, beaten

4 tbsp olive oil

150 ml (¼ pt) soured cream

150 ml (¼ pt) milk

This bread is risen with baking powder, making it quick to prepare. It is excellent with soup or Jambalaya (see recipe on page 87).

OVERLEAF • QUICK CHILLI BREAD

CHAPTER FIFTEEN
STOCKS

TIPS FOR MAKING PERFECT STOCK

1 • USE UNCOOKED BONES FREE FROM ANY FAT
AND BLOOD.

2 • USE NON-STARCHY VEGETABLES.

3 • COVER WITH COLD WATER.

4 • SKIM FREQUENTLY TO REMOVE FAT.

5 • DO NOT ALLOW TO BOIL, ONLY SIMMER.

6 • DO NOT STIR.

7 • DO NOT USE SALT.

BROWN MEAT STOCK

Pre-heat the oven to 220°C, 425°F, Gas 7.

Put the bones into a roasting tin and coat with 1 tbsp of oil. The tin should be large enough to hold the bones in a single layer. Brown the bones in the oven for 1 to 1½ hours.

In the meantime, cut the onion, carrot and celery into 5 cm (2in) chunks. Heat the rest of the oil in a sauté pan and fry the vegetables until golden brown. Take care not to burn them or the stock will be bitter.

Drain the fat from the bones and vegetables then place the bones and vegetables in a large saucepan with the remaining ingredients. Cover with 1 ltr (1¾ pt) cold water and bring to a simmer, skimming to remove the scum as it rises to the surface.

Adjust the heat so the surface of the liquid just trembles. Cook for 6 to 8 hours, skimming as required. Add additional cold water to the stock as needed to keep the bones and vegetables covered with liquid.

Strain the stock and discard the bones and vegetables. Boil the stock to reduce it by half for a well-flavoured stock. Cool, then store in the fridge for up to 2 days.

MAKES ABOUT 570 ML (1 PT)

225 g (8 oz) raw bones
2 tbsp oil
1 small onion
1 small carrot
1 celery stick, including the leaves
1 small tomato, chopped
4 mushrooms, chopped
2 fresh parsley stalks, lightly crushed
150 ml (¼ pt) red wine
1 bay leaf
1 sprig of thyme
½ tsp black peppercorns

A rich brown stock can be made with beef, veal, lamb or chicken bones, depending on the flavour required from the stock.

WHITE POULTRY OR

VEGETABLE STOCK

MAKES ABOUT 570 ML (1 PT)

1 raw poultry carcass
1 small onion, peeled and chopped
1 small carrot, chopped
1 celery stick, chopped
1 small leek, washed and chopped
2 fresh parsley stalks, lightly crushed
150 ml (¼ pt) white wine
1 bay leaf
½ tsp black peppercorns

To make a vegetable stock, leave out the carcass and double the quantities of vegetables.

Place all the ingredients in a large saucepan and cover with 1 ltr (1¾ pt) cold water.

Bring to the boil, skimming the scum from the surface as the water heats. As soon as the water starts to bubble turn the heat down so the liquid barely trembles.

Simmer for 3 to 4 hours then strain the stock into a clean saucepan and discard the bones and vegetables.

Boil the stock rapidly to reduce it by half for a well-flavoured stock. Cool then store in the fridge for up to 2 days.

FISH STOCK

MAKES ABOUT 570 ML (1 PT)

225 g (8 oz) raw fish bones and trimmings from a non-oily white fish such as sole, and/or prawn shells
1 small onion, peeled and chopped
1 small carrot, chopped
1 celery stick, chopped
1 small leek, washed and chopped
2 fresh parsley stalks, lightly crushed
150 ml (¼ pt) white wine
1 bay leaf
½ tsp black peppercorns

Bones from a non-oily white fish such as sole, or prawn shells, make the best-flavoured stock.

Cut the gills from the fish and discard. Rinse away any blood from the bones (blood will make the stock bitter.)

Place the bones and all the remaining ingredients into a large saucepan and cover with 1 ltr (1¾ pt) cold water.

Bring to the boil, skimming the scum from the surface as the water heats. As soon as the water starts to tremble, turn the heat down so the liquid barely simmers.

Simmer for 30 minutes then strain into a clean saucepan. Boil the stock rapidly to reduce by half for a well-flavoured stock.

Cool then store in the fridge for up to 2 days.

FOOD STORAGE AND HYGIENE

Although much of this advice will seem to be common sense, following safe food preparation and storage procedures is essential when preparing food in advance in order to prevent food-related illnesses.

Wash your hands thoroughly before working with food and in between food preparation tasks. Wash fruit and vegetables before and after peeling.

Ensure that work surfaces, chopping boards and utensils are clean before preparing food and clean them thoroughly in between food preparation tasks. Wash them with very hot water and detergent, rinse them well and dry them with a clean tea towel. If possible, use separate chopping boards for cooked and raw food.

Bacteria need warmth, moisture and time in order to multiply. Their favourite temperature is between 5°C and 60°C so keep food that needs to be refrigerated in the refrigerator for as long as possible and keep hot food hot. Check your refrigerator temperature; it should be between 1°C and 5°C. For storing food in a freezer as recommended in this book, the freezer temperature should be at -18°C (0°F).

When cooling food, place it in a shallow container with a wide surface area and stir it. Do not cover it. A large container of hot food can be cooled by placing the container in a sink of cold water. When the food is tepid, place it in the refrigerator. Do not let food normally stored in the refrigerator stand at room temperature for longer than 1½ hours. If in doubt about the safety of any food, throw it away.

Cover all food before storing it in the refrigerator to avoid different foods contaminating each other. Always place cooked food and dairy products on a higher shelf than raw meats and fish. Place these in the coldest part of your refrigerator. Follow the manufacturer's instructions about food storage as refrigerators differ.

Food for the freezer should be closely wrapped, then stored in plastic boxes or plastic bags specifically recommended for use in a freezer. Exclude as much air as possible from the container. Label clearly with the contents and the date of freezing. Defrost all frozen food in the refrigerator before cooking.

Do not reheat cooked food more than once. When reheating food, ensure it is piping hot right through to the centre before serving.

STORE CUPBOARD INGREDIENTS

Here is a list of useful ingredients that I always keep on hand in my kitchen.

almonds, ground
bay leaves
baking powder
bicarbonate of soda
black peppercorns
bouillon powder
cardamom pods
chilli powder
cinnamon, ground
cocoa powder
cumin, ground
couscous
cornflour
honey
flour: plain
    self-raising
    strong bread flour
gelatine

golden syrup
Madeira, dry
mustard: dry English
    wholegrain
    Dijon
olives
olive oil
pasta
pistachio nuts
rice: Arborio
    American
    Basmati
    Wild
saffron
sea salt
sesame oil
sugar: caster
    brown

sundried tomatoes
soy sauce
sunflower oil
tinned tomatoes
vanilla essence
vanilla pods
vinegar: Balsamic
    white wine
    red wine
Worchestershire sauce
yeast

SPECIALIST MAIL-ORDER SUPPLIERS

EMMETTS, PEASENHALL, SAXMUNDHAM, SUFFOLK, IP17 2HJ (01728 660250) SMOKED HAM AND BACON

FIDDES PAYNE LTD, UNIT 33, THORPE WAY, BANBURY, OXFORDSHIRE OX16 8XL (01295 253888) HERBS AND SPICES IN ALL FORMS AND ESSENTIAL OILS

FOX'S SPICES, UNITS J & K, MASONS ROAD INDUSTRIAL ESTATE, STRATFORD-UPON-AVON, WARWICKSHIRE CV37 9NF (01789 266420) SPICES, HERBS, MUSTARDS, PEPPERS AND ORIENTAL SPICES

GOODMAN'S GEESE, WALSGROVE FARM, GREAT WITLEY, WORCESTER WR6 6JJ (01299 896272) GEESE

JULIAN GRAVES LTD., HAM LANE, KINGSWINFORD, WEST MIDLANDS, DY6 7JH (01384 277772) DRIED EXOTIC FRUITS

L'AQUILA, 13-17 BARON STREET, LONDON, N1 9HN (0171 837 5555) TRUFFLES, DRIED MUSHROOMS AND SAFFRON

LINA'S, 18 BREWER STREET, LONDON W1R 3SS (0171 437 6482) HOME-MADE PASTA, BEANS, OLIVES, ITALIAN BREADS, PASTRIES, SALAMIS, CHEESES, DRIED MUSHROOMS

MARNEY MEATS, LAYER MARNEY TOWER, LAYER MARNEY, NR. COLCHESTER, ESSEX CO5 9US (01206 330784) VENISON, RARE BREAD PORK AND LAMB

ORIENTAL CITY, 399 EDGWARE ROAD, COLINDALE, LONDON NW9 0JJ (0181 200 0009) ALL TYPES OF FRESH AND CANNED JAPANESE FOODS

PINNEY'S OF ORFORD, MARKET HILL, ORFORD, WOODBRIDGE, SUFFOLK, IP12 2LH (01394 450277) SMOKED WILD AND FARMED SALMON

THE REAL MEAT COMPANY LTD., 51 MARKET PLACE, WARMINSTER, WILTSHIRE, BA12 9AZ (01985 219020) ORGANIC MEAT AND POULTRY

WILD OATS 210 WESTBOURNE GROVE, LONDON W11 2RH (0171 229 1063) HEALTH FOOD SHOP; ORGANIC FOODS

WING YIP, 395 EDGWARE ROAD, CRICKLEWOOD, LONDON NW2 6LN (0181 454 0422) ALL TYPES OF FRESH AND CANNED ORIENTAL FOODS

INDEX

mushrooms: cheat's wild mushroom
	risotto, 19
	Portabella mushroom salad, 43
	wild mushroom bread pudding, 102
mussels: jambalaya, 87
	salsa gratinéed mussels, 22

noodles, Thai, 115

onions: red onion focaccia, 182
orange: citrus jelly terrine, 122
	Sanguinello sorbet, 164
oysters Rockefeller, 21

pak choi and mangetout, stir-fried, *100*, 101
panettone chocolate chip bread pudding,
	135
panna cotta, chocolate, 131
Parmesan and chive scones, 179
Parmesan crisps, 46
passion fruit sauce, 167, *168*
pasta salad, green vegetable, 119
pâtés: herb cheese and cucumber, 34
	quick seafood, 38
pavlovas, pistachio, 136, *137*
pears, mulled wine, 130
pea and mint soup, iced, *12*, 13
pecan pie, maple, 142
peppers: red pepper and parsnip soup, 10
	roasted red pepper mousse, 35
pheasant braised with Madeira,
	pancetta and butterbeans, 62
pilaf, saffron rice and pasta, 117
pine nut macaroons, *124*, 125
pineapple, hot chilli, *160*, 161
pistachio pavlovas, 136, *137*
plum, pear and ginger sorbet, 163
pommes boulangére, 107
pommes Dauphinoise, 111
pork: cheese-crusted chops, *72*, 73
	curried pork fillet and red pepper
		sauté, 78
	mu-shu pork, 40
	pork fillet stuffed with Toulouse sausages
		and prunes, 71
	pork fillet with wholegrain mustard sauce,
		74
	pork fillet with wild mushrooms en
		croûte, 75
Portabella mushroom salad, 43
potatoes, 105-12
	garlic and olive oil mashed potatoes, 109
	pommes boulangére, 107
	pommes Dauphinoise, 111

sautéed new potatoes, 108
	spicy potato wedges, 107
	two-potato galette, 110
poultry stock, 188
poussin, lemon and herb-crusted, 63
prawns: Chinese tiger prawn and
	mangetout salad, 48
	prawn and avocado pasta, 94
	tiger prawn, celeriac and apple soup, 11

raspberry coulis, 165
red mullet roasted with broad bean purée,
	90
red snapper baked with herbs, 91
rhubarb and blueberry strudel, 151
rice: cheat's wild mushroom risotto, 19
	jambalaya, 87
	risotto tomatoes, 99
	saffron rice and pasta pilaf, 117
	sesame rice, 118
	Thai rice salad, 118
rocket and spinach salad, 47
rolls, 170-1
rosti, sweet potato, 112
roulade, toasted almond, *144*, 145

saffron rice and pasta pilaf, 117
salads, 41-8, 55, 101, 104, 114, 116, 118-19
salmon: fillets with a pistachio crust, 92, 93
	soy marinated whole salmon, *88, 89*
	vodka-cured salmon, 39
salsa gratinéed mussels, 22
salsas, 68, 93
Sanguinello sorbet, 164
scallops, grilled with chilli and garlic, 20
scones, Parmesan and chive, 179
sea bass, sweet chilli, 96
seafood: quick seafood pâté, 38
	seafood lasagne, 86
sesame bread sticks, 174
sesame rice, 118
smoked cod and asparagus, 18
sorbets, 158, 163-4
soufflés, 23, 27, 129
soups, 9-16
soy-braised guinea fowl, 59
soy marinated whole salmon, *88, 89*
spinach: double-baked spinach and sage
soufflés, 23
	spinach and lentil soup, 14
stocks, 185-8
strawberries: strawberry and mascarpone
	tart, 152, 153
	strawberry tiramisu, 138

toasted almond roulade with, *144*, 145

strudel, rhubarb and blueberry, 151
succotash, 103
summer berry sorbet, 158
sweet potatoes: candied sweet potatoes, 110
	sweet potato rosti, 112
	two-potato galette, 110
sweetcorn: succotash, 103
	sweetcorn and red pepper salsa, 93
	sweetcorn pancakes, 18

tabbouleh, 114
tarts: brûléed crab tartlets, 30
	chocolate and cinnamon tart, 154
	maple pecan pie, 142
	mincemeat tart, *148, 149*
	sticky fruit tart, 146
	strawberry and mascarpone tart, *152, 153*
Thai green curry chicken salad, 55
Thai noodles, 115
Thai rice salad, 118
Thai-style crab cakes, 28, *29*
tiramisu, strawberry, 138
tomatoes: risotto tomatoes, 99
	roasted tomato soup, 16
	tomato, mint and courgette salsa, 68
tropical citrus salad, 123
tuiles, lime and coconut, 127
tuna: turkey tonnato, 50
turkey: fresh roast turkey with a herby
	sausage stuffing, 51
	turkey tonnato, 50

veal noisettes with peppers, 83, *84*
vegetables, 97-104
	glazed spring vegetables, 102
	green vegetable pasta salad, 119
	grilled vegetable and goat's cheese stacks,
	31, *32*
	vegetable stock, 188
venison casserole with sour cherries and
	port, 82
vodka-cured salmon, 39

watercress and spinach soup, 15
wholemeal refrigerator bread, *177*, 178
wine: mulled wine pears, 130

zabaglione, Amaretto and apricot, *124*, 125